CLEMENTE

A CELEBRA BOOK

THE CLEMENTE FAMILY

THE TRUE LEGACY OF AN UNDYING HERO

CLEMENTE

Celebra
Published by the Penguin Group
Penguin Group (USA) Inc., 375 Hudson Street,
New York, New York 10014, USA

USA | Canada | UK | Ireland | Australia | New Zealand | India | South Africa | China

Penguin Books Ltd., Registered Offices: 80 Strand, London WC2R 0RL, England
For more information about the Penguin Group visit penguin.com.

First published by Celebra,
a division of Penguin Group (USA) Inc.

First Printing, October 2013

LIBRARY OF CONGRESS CATALOGING-IN-PUBLICATION DATA:
Clemente family
Clemente: the true legacy of an undying hero/The Clemente Family.
p. cm.
Includes bibliographical references.
ISBN 978-0-451-41903-3
1. Clemente, Roberto, 1934–1972. 2. Clemente, Roberto, 1934–1972—Family. 3. Clemente, Roberto,
1934–1972—Death and burial. 4. Clemente family—Interviews. 5. Baseball players—Puerto Rico—Biography.
6. Humanitarians—United States—Biography. I. Title.
GV865.C45C54 2013
796.357092—dc23   2013017078
[B]

Printed in China
10 9 8 7 6 5 4 3 2 1

Set in Spectrum MT Std
Designed by Pauline Neuwirth

To Vera Clemente . . .
who continues to represent her family and the sport of baseball
with dignity and class

Contents

| INTRODUCTION |
THEIR STORY
1

| CHAPTER ONE |
LOVE
11

| CHAPTER TWO |
SACRIFICE
43

| CHAPTER THREE |
MEMORIES
69

| CHAPTER FOUR |
"A MAN OF HONOR PLAYED BASEBALL HERE"
105

| CHAPTER FIVE |
HOMBRE INVISIBLE
135

| CHAPTER SIX |
EMERGENCE
163

| CHAPTER SEVEN |
PREMONITIONS
189

| CHAPTER EIGHT |
ETERNAL
219

| EPILOGUE |
21
249

Acknowledgments
259

Notes
261

Bibliography
262

CLEMENTE

THEIR STORY

"If you have a chance to accomplish something that will

make things better for people coming behind you, and you

don't do that, you are wasting your time on this Earth."

—Roberto Clemente

As a young journalist, I once asked Muhammad Ali who were the athletes he admired the most. It didn't take long for him to mention Roberto Clemente. "I think the greatest thing you can say about a person," Ali said, "is that they gave their life for their cause. That's what Roberto Clemente did. He was a beautiful human being."

Roberto Clemente spent his life helping others and died while doing so. He was dedicated to family, baseball, and aiding, in many cases, total strangers. Before the modern era of slick publicists, Twitter, and Facebook, Clemente empowered the poor and downtrodden with little acclaim. He died in a plane crash forty years ago while en route to help the Nicaraguan people who had been devastated by an earthquake. The plane was overloaded with tons of supplies.

Clemente was one of my childhood heroes. I was deeply affected by the fact that he gave his life trying to help others. There was also my admiration for what I considered his vastly underrated athletic ability, generated with nothing but spit and hard work. Clemente achieved a level of strength and speed—especially in his throwing arm—that only a handful of other players reached in the presteroid era. He was in the same talent class as contemporaries Willie Mays and Mickey Mantle.

Clemente has been called the Latino Jackie Robinson. He was the first Latin player elected to the Baseball Hall of Fame, the first to win a World Series title as a starter, a World Series MVP, and an MVP award. The more appropriate Clemente comparison isn't Robinson but Lou Gehrig. They were two baseball greats lost long before their time—Clemente in an accident and Gehrig from a deadly disease. Gehrig was the first baseball player to have the Hall of Fame's five-year waiting period waived. Clemente was the second. Clemente died at the age of thirty-eight, and Gehrig said his iconic good-bye to baseball when he was thirty-seven.

One of Clemente's former Pirates managers, the late Bobby Bragan, said that when he heard about Clemente's death, he had the same pit in his stomach as when he first learned of the assassination of President John F. Kennedy.

Clemente overcame great racism in the post-Robinson era, which remained a brutal time in American history for athletes of color, despite Robinson's groundbreaking achievement. The bigotry of the time—early in Clemente's career he couldn't stay in the same hotels as some of his white teammates—prevented many fans and some of the writers who covered him from seeing the truth about Clemente, who, in addition to being an artistic baseball player, also studied ceramics, wrote poetry, and played music. He was intensely loyal. Clemente had a saying: "Never lie to me, and we'll always be friends."

In the early 1980s, television producer Maury Gable attempted to get a film made about Clemente's life. Gable created a TV movie about Pittsburgh Steelers running back Rocky Bleier's comeback from wounds he received fighting in the Vietnam War. He found Clemente's story of athleticism, grace, and sacrifice to be equally compelling. But Gable ran into a problem. "The networks weren't interested in a movie about a Puerto Rican ballplayer," he said. So, even then, more than ten years after his death, many aspects of mainstream America didn't fully comprehend Clemente's importance in sports history.

It remains highly interesting that all these decades later, in a sports movie industry that cherishes films about the underdog—*Rocky*, *Rudy*, *Miracle*, and *Hoosiers* to name a few—no movie about another underdog in Clemente has been made.

In the Latino community, then and now, Clemente is more than cherished. He remains genuinely loved. When Ozzie Guillen was a shortstop for the Chicago White Sox, he kept an altar to Clemente in his home, complete with pictures and statuettes. Go to any ballpark in the world and the Clemente name is still admired.

The anniversary of his death, which will result in the celebration of his life, comes at an interesting time in sports history. Never before in sports has the genuineness of athletes—their performances on the field and what they do off of it—been questioned as deeply as now.

What the life of Clemente taught us was that his era, though complicated with issues of race and power, was simple in one big way: You could believe your eyes. There was no human growth hormone in Clemente's blood. Just humanness.

Most of my life has been spent studying and writing about sports history, and to me, Clemente represents the greatest combination of athlete and humanitarian who ever lived.

The things that have been said about Clemente over the years remain remarkable. "Roberto Clemente was the best unorthodox player this game has ever seen," said

Don Baylor, who has been a major-league player or manager since 1970, and won the 1985 Roberto Clemente Award. "The thing that made him special was the results. He said, 'I believe we owe something to the people who watch us play.'"

"Clemente was bigger than life as far as his arm was concerned," said Tim McCarver, who played against Clemente for more than ten years. "What made it unique with Roberto was his whirl and throw. He would actually field the ball off the carom in that short, but very difficult Forbes Field wall, catch it, pivot on the back foot, and turn and throw almost blindly at times."

"He made the greatest throws I ever saw in my life," former major leaguer Rusty Staub said. "He would go into that bull pen [near the right-field line in Forbes Field] where you couldn't see home plate. One time, he went for a ball that spun into the bull pen. A guy was tagging up from third base with one out. He knew he had it made; he didn't run hard. All of a sudden this rocket came from nowhere. It was like a strike, right across the plate. He [Clemente] couldn't even see home plate."

"I looked at Roberto pretty much the way I looked at my dad: as someone who was invincible, someone that would always be there," said former Pirates teammate Al Oliver.

Clemente's significance can still be measured: in the tiny ballparks from the United States to Puerto Rico and many other parts of Latin America; in the major-league stadiums that still feel his import; in the stadium in Puerto Rico that still bears his name; in the words of two U.S. presidents across several decades who honored him; in the award named for him and presented by baseball yearly to players who are special on the field and charitable off of it; and, perhaps most of all, how his widow, Vera, continues his legacy with honor and humility.

I spent months with the Clemente family—Vera, and three sons, Roberto Jr., Luis, and Ricky—listening to their stories about a great husband, father, and friend. Ricky, in fact, submitted to his first-ever interview. (Some family members, and close friends called Roberto by his nickname, Momen, but for the sake of clarity I have them using his formal name for this book. The nickname, says Clemente's only surviving brother, eighty-five-year-old Justino Clemente Walker, comes from when Roberto was a child. Family members would call to Clemente and he'd always reply, "*Momentito*"; Momentito became Momen. Justino, meanwhile, looks like a man in his fifties, and his memory remains sharp.)

The family has continued their father's life of selflessness, and done so in classy Clemente form. In two decades of practicing journalism, I have never met a more sincere and decent group of people. In a short period of time, I came to cherish them.

This book is their memory of a man they knew better than anyone. This is their story as told to me.

Many of the stories they tell have not been heard before. This is what makes their book unique, because it's a view of their father directly from their eyes, minds, and hearts. Some of the photographs in this book have also never been seen before.

Other parts of the book contain interviews from friends of the Clemente family and former teammates, and previous interviews from other journalistic sources, including books, magazines, and daily newspaper articles from both the United States and Puerto Rico spanning four decades. They are all properly credited.

Not long after Clemente's death, a nun from Pittsburgh who was a teacher at the San Antonio Catholic School in Río Piedras, Puerto Rico, told her student that God had wanted Roberto Clemente's resting place to be in the ocean so that he could spread across the universe. Vera found out about this thanks to Lourdes Berrios, her beloved neightbor's daughter, because she was a student at the school. That is how Clemente affected people—then and now.

There is no greater example of Clemente's generosity and dedication than the fact his life ended while he was on a mission of mercy.

"He loved the game and he was always trying to stress to his contemporaries that it was a game you have to dedicate yourself to," Clemente's friend Luis Mayoral once said. ". . . [H]e had the mind of a philosopher. He had the fire within him, a lot of pride, but it was not the kind of pride that would ever allow him to downgrade another individual. I like to think of him in terms of his hands. He had strong hands, the claws of a tiger. He had ferocity in his hands, but they were the same hands who would pat the heads of the children. He created a conscience related to the strugglers: the guy in the factory in Pittsburgh, the guy in the factory in Puerto Rico, the taxi driver, the nine-to-five guy. His sense of pride was their sense of pride. I think he would still be in the game somehow, but I see him [as] more of a sociologist, not necessarily a politician. He was trying to help people better themselves."

In the 1994 All-Star game in Pittsburgh, a bronze statue of Clemente was revealed, created mostly thanks to funds donated by the Pittsburgh players. One of them was Orlando Merced, who grew up across the street from Clemente in Puerto Rico. He told *Sports Illustrated* then: "Roberto Clemente means a dream to me, and to a lot of kids and people. I never met him, but I played baseball inside his house, around the Gold Gloves, the silver bats, the trophies, the pictures. He has pushed me to be a better player and a better person. When they unveiled the statue, I was crying. It made me proud to be who I am and to be a Puerto Rican."

"When I put on my uniform," Clemente once said, "I feel I am the proudest man on Earth."

"He gave the term 'complete' a new meaning. He made the word 'superstar' seem inadequate. He had about him the touch of royalty."—Baseball Commissioner Bowie Kuhn (1973 eulogy).

—MIKE FREEMAN

CHAPTER ONE

LOVE

I see him all the time. I see him mostly in his quiet moments. Sometimes he's play-ing with the kids. Sometimes he's laughing. He was a great husband to me. He was a great father. He wrote poetry. I called him Roberto.

We met in a drugstore in Carolina, Puerto Rico. I was working at a bank. One af-ternoon, I went out to buy something at the drugstore. When I got there, Roberto was sitting in a chair, reading the newspaper. He looked up. It was like something from a movie. I knew who he was and I was a little starstruck. He asked my name, I told him, and then I started to leave. He said, "Don't leave." That was how we met. He had a very kind smile.

I came from a strict family. I was shy, and when he first asked me for a date I said no. He had his niece call me at the bank, and I'm not sure why, but that made me say yes.

He came to the Banco Gubernamental de Fomento, where I used to work, to take me out to lunch. He waited outside. The employees went outside, two at a time, to see him. We went to lunch at the Caribe Hilton and I could see he was sincerely interested

OCT • 66

in me. He was dressed in a suit. He drove a white Cadillac and opened the door for me to get in. I was nervous and pressed tight against the [passenger-side] car door. He was very kind.

After that, he went home to his mother and said he'd found the girl he was going to marry. He was romantic that way. The first time he came to my home, Roberto said he was going to marry me. A few dates later, he brought pictures of houses. He also brought a diamond ring. He wanted to marry quickly, because he had to get to spring training very soon. [She laughs.]

My father was not convinced. We were married on November 14, 1964.

He planned everything fast, because he used to always say, "I'm going to die young."

Roberto was a great baseball player, but he was a great father and husband. He also could do many other things. He could write poetry. I remember a Father's Day game in Pittsburgh, and he was in full uniform. He was writing on the back of a piece of paper. It was poem. It was called "*¿Quién Soy?*"—"Who Am I?"

Who Am I?

I am a small point in the eye of the full moon.

I only need one ray of the sun to warm my face.

I only need one breeze from the

Alisios to refresh my soul.

What else can I ask if I know that my

sons really love me?

I loved him so much.

There was a time in November, not long before the crash, when Roberto woke up in the middle of the night. I remember him saying, "I just had a very strange dream. I was sitting in the clouds, watching my own funeral."

The last time I saw him, he was boarding the plane. He stood in the doorway of the plane and looked back to me. He had a very sad look. I'll never forget that look.

VERA CLEMENTE: He loved baseball since he was a child. I think that's all he ever wanted to do. He wanted to be a great baseball player.

LUIS CLEMENTE (son): My dad was a happy guy, but he was very happy when he was with his family, and happy when he was playing baseball.

ROBERTO CLEMENTE JR. (son): He was a kind man and a great dad, so it was always strange to hear and later read about how ruthless he was as a baseball player.

CLEMENTE

RICKY CLEMENTE (son): Through his actions, Dad taught us to treat people the way you want to be treated. He taught us to be kind to everyone and not care about a person's color. That message stuck with all of us.

ROBERTO CLEMENTE, 1961: I am between the worlds. So anything I do will reflect on me because I am black and . . . will reflect on me because I am Puerto Rican. To me, I always respect everybody. And thanks to God, when I grow up, I was raised . . . my mother and father never told me to hate anyone, or they never told me to dislike anyone because of racial color. We never talked about that.

VERA: Right before the [plane] accident, he was supposed to give a baseball clinic to kids in Puerto Rico. He did that all the time. His sons saw things like that and tried to be like their dad in that way. [The field where Clemente gave many of those clinics still exists in Puerto Rico.]

JUSTINO CLEMENTE WALKER (Clemente's eighty-five-year-old

brother): Roberto rarely took time for himself. His time was for others, his
family, strangers. Only time he did something for himself was after the season. He'd go to a farm he owned near the [El Yunque] rain forest. He'd just relax. If the Pirates weren't in the World Series, he'd relax on that farm and
watch the World Series on television. He once spent the day with Martin Luther King in his other farm in Martin González in Carolina. They talked
about everything. Roberto admired how [King] gave poor people a voice.

LUIS MAYORAL ON CLEMENTE AND KING: They became friends. I do remember that around 1970 there was an All-Star game—it could have been
sixty-nine—in Los Angeles at Dodgers Stadium, where blacks and Latinos
played to raise funds for the Martin Luther King foundation. And one of the
most prized possessions or awards that Roberto got was a Martin Luther King
medallion for playing in that game.

ROBERTO CLEMENTE, 1970: When Martin Luther King started doing what he did, he changed the whole system of the American style. He put the people, the ghetto people, the people who didn't have nothing to say in those days, they started saying what they would have liked to say for many years that nobody listened to. Now, with this man, these people come down to the place where they were supposed to be, but people didn't want them, and sit down as if they were white and call attention to whole world. Now, that wasn't only the black people, but the minority people. The people who didn't have anything, and they had nothing to say in those days because they didn't have any power; they started saying things and they started picketing, and that's the reason I say [King] changed the world. . . .

HEAD PIRATES TRAINER TONY BARTIROME: I met Roberto in spring training. It was 1955. That was my first year with the Pirates as a player [he later became the Pirates' trainer from 1967 to 1985]. I clicked with him immediately. He had this sense of social justice. He was genuinely confused by the bigotry he saw in America.

TEAMMATE STEVE BLASS: What Roberto did, especially toward the latter part of his

career, was help to unify a locker room that had become increasingly diverse, and it became increasingly diverse because of Roberto.

TEAMMATE AL OLIVER: Our conversations always stemmed around people from all walks of life being able to get along well, no excuse why it shouldn't be. . . . He had a problem with people who treated you differently because of where you were from, your nationality, your color, also poor people, how they were treated. . . . That's the thing I really respected about him most, was his character, the things he believed in.

TONY BARTIROME: He talked about change a lot. Changing baseball to make it better for the Latin and black player. He saw that as his small way of changing the country for the better.

LUIS CLEMENTE: I remember watching my father on a documentary and he was saying how he wanted the kids to grow up not spoiled and he wanted us to suffer. I remember watching that and going, "Why would he want his sons to suffer? I don't want my kids to suffer." But later I understood what he meant. He didn't want us to literally suffer. He didn't want us to live off the Clemente name. Dad didn't want us to be these rich kids. He wanted us to be humble, to never forget where we came from. He wanted us to work as hard as he did, and when you watch him play baseball, and read about his work ethic, he worked really hard. He lived the life of a humble man.

RICKY CLEMENTE: Being his son was not difficult. It was great. People don't really know who I am unless I say my name; then they ask about my dad. The biggest thing I think Dad wanted us to do was work hard and follow our own path. Treat people well, the way he did.

JUSTINO CLEMENTE WALKER: When he was young, in Puerto Rico, Roberto was left off one of the All-Star teams. [Former Dodgers executive] Al Campanis was in Puerto Rico and heard about it. Campanis said, "That had to be a great team, because they left the greatest player in all of Puerto Rico off of it." Roberto used not being named to that All-Star team as motivation. It made him work even harder.

VERA CLEMENTE: He taught our sons by example. They learned about work ethic from watching Roberto. He was tough. He was hard to keep down. I think he really started to feel comfortable after a few years with the Pirates. I think around 1956 he started to really adjust to being in Pittsburgh.

ROBERTO CLEMENTE JR.: At one point, Dad was hitting everything. That year was really the beginning of what kind of player he'd become.

EARLY DURING THE 1956 season—only his second in the big leagues—Clemente hit one home run a day for eight consecutive days. By early June, the Pirates had crawled to first place, and Clemente was third in baseball with a .357 average. The Pirates would eventually slide out of first, but Clemente was beginning to smash major-league pitching. Yet he was still dealing with portions of a press corps that portrayed him as a malingerer. Some of the writers that covered the team didn't understand that many of Clemente's ailments were real—aches and pains forged in a frightening car accident leading to serious back trauma.

Clemente pushed through his injuries because he believed he had a higher purpose: He wanted to use baseball to energize Puerto Rican children, to teach them to believe they could become great as well—either in sports or in everyday life.

He expressed this once, saying, in part, "To me, I don't want to accomplish some-

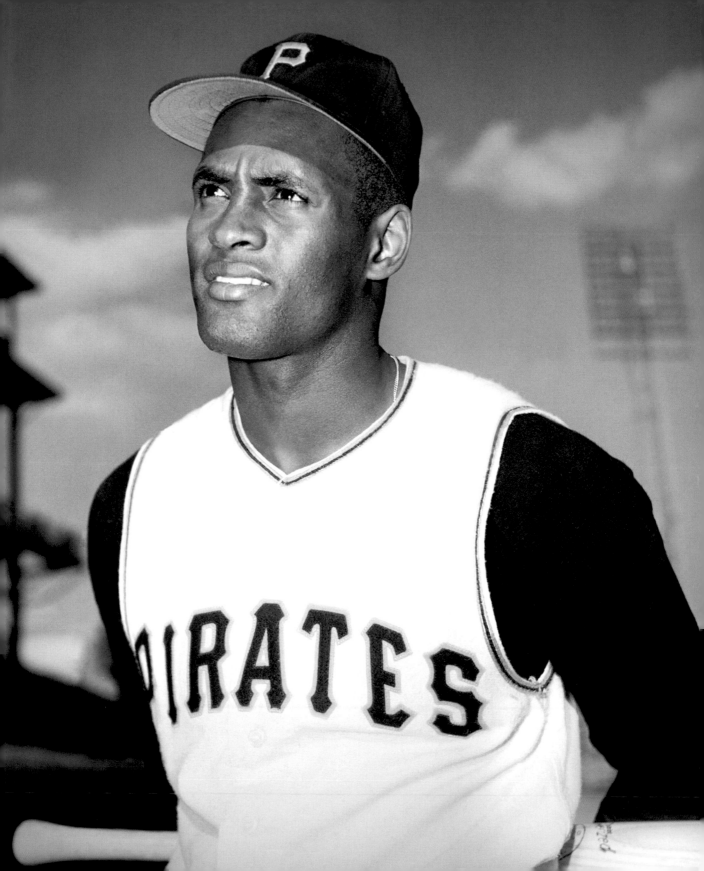

CLEMENTE

thing so I can be able to say, 'Hey, look at me; look at what I did.' I want to accomplish something for life."

Mantle would also suffer from a number of injuries, but he was hailed as a hero by the press for pushing through them. Said Clemente, "Mickey Mantle is God, but if a Latin or black is sick, they say it is in his head."

Though Clemente's battles with the press would become intense, something became clear to many of the writers who covered him. "One thing stood out," Pirates beat writer Ira Miller was quoted as saying in 1972; "through all of the outbursts and the arguments and controversies, it was almost impossible not to like the guy. I can remember the first time as a rookie that I had to interview him. He was polite and pleasant, as though he sensed my anxiety and was trying to make it easier for me. If the question was particularly penetrating, he might sit there for a moment with that quizzical, little-boy look on his face. But always there was an answer, and always it came from the heart."

JUSTINO CLEMENTE WALKER: People used to say he was a [hypochondriac]. But he was tough. He played through a lot of painful things. The American press didn't understand that. He played with so much pain. Once, when I saw him and said hi, I lightly tapped his elbow. He winced and pulled his elbow away. There was a lot of calcification. In 1965, he traveled to the Dominican Republic. He got really sick, and it took doctors two weeks to figure out that he had malaria. He got so sick, we all wondered if he'd ever play baseball again.

VERA CLEMENTE: His temperature was 105 degrees. He lost twenty pounds. His doctor told him he should sit out [the 1965 season] because he had been so sick.

TONY BARTIROME: I don't think I've ever met a tougher guy. He was arthritic in his neck. He was constantly in pain. I was always working on him to ease the pain, and he pushed through it. He wasn't a hypochondriac. He was a fighter.

ROBERTO CLEMENTE JR.: With all the injuries he had, I don't know how he was such a good player. He was genuinely hurt. A lot of his physical issues came from the car accident.

LUIS CLEMENTE: The car accident was the huge source of his back problems.

VERA CLEMENTE: His back was always hurting. I was always massaging it and working the pressure points. After games, his back would get really sore. But he always tried to play.

JUSTINO CLEMENTE WALKER: I was in the car with Roberto when the accident happened. It was 1954. We were coming from Ponce to go visit our brother, who was very ill. The light turned green and we started to drive. Car went through a red light and came straight at us. [The driver was drunk and slammed into Clemente's car at sixty miles per hour. The impact damaged three of Clemente's spinal disks, causing him back pain for the rest of his career.] Roberto saw the car coming and tensed up. His back was really hurt. The accident happened on December thirtieth. Our brother died on December thirty-first.

THE 1960 SEASON. It would change everything for Clemente. Pittsburgh would become one of the more unlikely champions in the history of baseball, beating the storied and heavily favored New York Yankees in the World Series. The Pirates would win twenty-one of their games that season in the ninth inning, twelve when the team faced two outs.

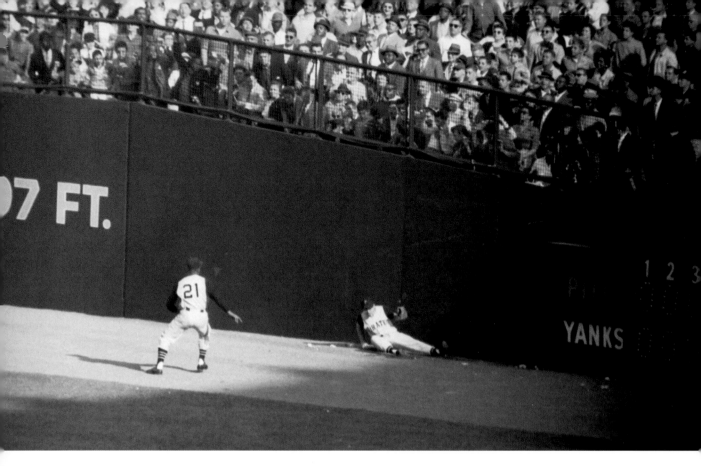

Roberto Clemente was the catalyst. His 1960 campaign marked the beginning of stunning performances in huge moments—the true definition of greatness. By May, he led the National League with a .353 batting average and had already thrown out nineteen base runners. There was a pivotal moment that occurred during the season that perfectly illustrated Clemente's abilities and mental sturdiness. It came in a game at Forbes Field against the San Francisco Giants. Willie Mays hit one pitch down the right-field line, the baseball sailing away from Clemente at an impossible speed, as he trailed in a flurry of speed and aggression. As Clemente caught the ball he smashed into a concrete obstruction. The crash led to a cut across Clemente's jaw, and as he raised his glove to show the catch was made, the crowd and blood from his chin both erupted.

Clemente would later exhibit other combinations of footwork and courage that were equally amazing. One came inside the Houston Astrodome in 1971. The Pirates were leading 1–0 in the bottom of the eighth inning, with two outs. Joe Morgan was on first base, and Bob Watson was at the plate. Watson hit a pitch not so dissimilar from the one Mays crushed. The ball started to severely slice toward the right-field corner, and Clemente was in hard pursuit. It seemed a matter of certainty that Clemente would slow to avoid running into the outfield fence. He didn't. His body fully extended and his back to home plate, Clemente snagged the ball just as it was about to clear for a home run, then crashed into the fence and hit the ground. It was such an impressive play that the more than sixteen thousand Houston fans gave Clemente a standing ovation. The result of the collision with the fence was Clemente slicing his left knee, bruising his left elbow, and injuring his left ankle. Since the game wasn't on television, it was never recorded, and thus never widely seen.

Clemente went into the hospital to get the wound stitched. The Pirates had a seven-game lead over Milwaukee. When he emerged after five days of medical treatment, the team's lead had shrunk to two games.

On September 25, the Pirates won the pennant, and the city of Pittsburgh won its first championship in more than three decades.

PEOPLE WERE CATCHING on, albeit slowly, about just how good Clemente was. One of the first glaring aspects of his game was his stance. His bat, thirty-six ounces and almost cartoonish in its massive size, took huge swings. Clemente's footwork wasn't traditional; instead of stepping inward to attack the pitch, he would move his left foot inside or out, depending on the ball's location. This would allow him great power and maneuverability. "Pitch me outside," Clemente once explained, "and I will hit four hundred. Pitch me inside, and you will not find the ball."

Asked how to pitch to Clemente, Hall of Famer Sandy Koufax said, "Roll the ball."

Clemente entered the 1960 World Series against the Yankees a confident but particularly agitated man. He had hoped to win the Most Valuable Player award of the National League. He had earned it: His bat powered the Pirates to a postseason spot not many had predicted, and, in just 132 games, Clemente finished the regular season at .341 with eighty-six RBIs. Yet it was becoming clear that Pirates teammate Dick Groat was going to win the award.

Not only did Clemente fail to win the MVP, he finished eighth behind Groat. Clemente received one first-place vote. Thus the baseball writers regarded Clemente as the eighth most vital player in all of baseball and the fourth most valuable Pirate.

JUSTINO CLEMENTE WALKER: He always resented being voted eighth. It always bothered him, years after it happened. He never forgot it. It motivated him for the rest of his career. If you doubted Roberto, he always proved you wrong.

VERA CLEMENTE: It really hurt him. He was shocked. He was not upset with [Groat]. He was upset with where he was voted. It was motivation for him.

LUIS CLEMENTE: It seems like there was always someone doubting my dad, and then he'd just get better and better.

VERA CLEMENTE: What made Roberto so good at baseball was that he was the same all the time. After a [regular season] game, we'd come home, and I'd cook dinner for him. He'd relax and we would eat and talk. After the World Series games, it was the same. He was very level. This helped him be a great player, because he never changed his personality.

I remember when he got his three thousandth hit. He was very excited about it. We had a group of friends from Puerto Rico who had been following him from game to game when he got close to three thousand. We went back to the apartment and the parking lot was full of cars. I know he wanted to just have some time alone with the family but wanted to be gracious to everyone.

CLEMENTE

JUSTINO CLEMENTE WALKER: When Roberto was younger, he was a very strong hitter, but pitchers would jam him. When he was with [the Puerto Rican minor-league team] Santurce, [the coaches] tried to restrict his foot movement and change his stance. They put an obstacle near his left foot that kept it from moving. Roberto hurt his ankle knocking it against the obstacle. Thankfully they never changed his stance. He wouldn't let them. He knew it worked for him. That was Roberto. If he knew he was right, you couldn't change his mind. Not even his family could change it. He was strong mentally.

I remember 1960. Roberto was so determined to win a championship. He thought it was the [Pirates'] time. He wanted to prove to people he wasn't some of the things they were saying about him. Roberto wanted to show that the Puerto Rican player could win big games. I think some people thought the Puerto Rican player wasn't as good as other players.

LUIS CLEMENTE: I think he also wanted to show he was as good as Willie Mays.

JUSTINO CLEMENTE WALKER: He was proud of that catch [on Mays's hit], but it hurt a lot. [She laughs.] He needed a lot of stitches.

When he came home [to Puerto Rico] after beating the Yankees, he came to the airport, and there were thousands of fans waiting for him. He hugged all of us [family members]. Then the crowd picked him up and carried him on their shoulders.

CLEMENTE WOULD OVERCOME the sting of his eighth-place finish and, more than a decade later, emerge victorious from a dramatic chase to three thousand hits, something he accomplished on the last weekend of the 1972 season. It was actually the last baseball game he'd ever play. The first Latino to reach that mark, he was also only the eleventh player in history to do so. Along the way came two World Series titles, a World Series Most Valuable Player award, a regular-season MVP in 1966, four batting titles, and twelve Gold Glove awards (the latter coming in each of his last twelve seasons). By the time Clemente's career had ended he'd played in more games, had more RBIs, more at-bats, more hits, singles, and total bases than any player in Pirates history. Clemente achieved all of this by the age of thirty-eight.

Clemente was a key component in one of baseball's great ages, with names like Mays, Aaron, and Mantle, and was as physically gifted as any of them. In fact, his .317 lifetime batting average was higher than the batting averages of all three of those legends. The Pirates won both of their seven-game World Series in large part because of Clemente hitting safely in all fourteen of those games.

In 1971, Clemente was one of the game's most fearsome players. He hit .341 for the year as Pittsburgh won the pennant. Yet he was still largely overlooked by the national media, something that would change in the World Series against Baltimore. Decades earlier, as a player in the premier amateur league in Puerto Rico, Clemente had demonstrated an impressive ability to throw out base runners from deep center field. Now his arm was again on display as he engaged in one of the more stunning performances in championship history. What's more, he hit .414 and was voted the series MVP.

In the clubhouse after Game 7, he was asked to speak a few words. He said that before speaking in English, he wanted to say something in Spanish: *"En el dia mas grande de mi vida a los nenes la bendición mía, y que mis padres me echen la bendición en Puerto Rico."* The English translation is "In the greatest day of my life, my blessings go to the kids, and my parents bless me in Puerto Rico." These were the first words ever spoken in Spanish live via satellite.

Clemente attracted the attention of essayist Roger Angell, one of the elite sportswriters of the period, who penned numerous baseball pieces in *The New Yorker* magazine. There wasn't a greater symbol of Clemente's arrival into America's living room than the Harvard-educated Angell chronicling Clemente's World Series exploits. Before Game 7, Clemente told Angell: "I want everybody in the world to know that this is the way I play all the time. All season, every season, I gave everything I had to this game."

Angell wrote in his 1972 book *The Summer Game*: "There was . . . Clemente playing a kind of baseball that none of us had seen before—throwing and running and hitting at something close to the level of absolute perfection, playing to win but also playing the game almost as if it were a form of punishment for everyone else on the field."

STORIES LIKE ANGELL'S were important, because they weren't just an acknowledgment of Clemente; they were an endorsement. Angell provided a permission slip for fans to be enthralled. But despite his reaching such heights, in some ways there remained a lack of appreciation for Clemente. *Sports Illustrated* informed Clemente that he would be on the cover of the magazine when he reached three thousand hits. It wasn't Clemente who appeared on the cover, however, but Joe Namath. Even in Pittsburgh, which has always celebrated the achievements of its local stars with as much fervor as any city, the main local newspaper didn't lead with Clemente's three thousandth hit. It led the sports section with a loss by the Pittsburgh Panthers college football team.

Yet some were indeed enthralled, like Commissioner Bowie Kuhn, who called Clemente baseball royalty.

Few understood just how impactful Clemente would become, or that he was far more multidimensional as a person than anyone outside of his family or close friends fully understood. He followed national politics intently and spoke openly about his disgust that hunger and want still existed in such a wealthy nation. He committed acts of kindness with no public relations officials present, and outside of precharity press conferences.

When Clemente would film commercials and endorsements in Puerto Rico, he'd take the money, sometimes tens of thousands of dollars, and donate it to various charities in cities across the area. On "Roberto Clemente Night" in 1970, a day dedicated to honoring Clemente, he was given $6,000 by the team, the equivalent of about $33,000 today. He gave that money to a children's hospital in Pittsburgh. At the time, few knew. Clemente would take bags full of coins and hand them to poor people he'd seek out in the street. He provided most of the $700 needed to provide the prosthetic legs for a wheelchair-bound twelve-year-old boy. Hospital visits were numerous and almost never publicized. "Days before doctors would operate, they'd ask my dad to speak to the patients," Luis said. A year before the plane crash Clemente was planning to open a modest chiropractic center in Puerto Rico.

Clemente went into hospital rooms unannounced, the patients suddenly smiling as if a deity had entered.

Clemente was one of the first professional athletes to fully understand that power and wealth didn't have to transform just a single individual. They could act as engines to alter the lives of many. Once Clemente fully embraced this belief, the course of his life would change forever, and so would that of his family. "Eventually what my father saw was that he could use baseball, and the fame generated by baseball, to help people in big ways," says Roberto Jr.

One year before the plane crash Clemente planned to open a modest medical facility in Puerto Rico not far from their home. Vera was going to assist him. There would be a few more years of baseball, and then family and a career of healing others. Clemente's life was becoming firmly settled.

CLEMENTE SPENT THREE weeks in Nicaragua earlier in 1972, and as he had done in many places, he met a number of people he came to like. Three days before Christmas, Clemente and Vera awoke in Puerto Rico to news of a series of earthquakes that had flattened the city of Managua, leaving it in ruins.

"I remember my father being extremely sad," Roberto says, "and then there was a lot of activity around the house. You knew something big was about to happen."

"Dad was communicating with a ham radio operator in Managua," says Luis, "and he was asking, 'What do you need?' The city was destroyed. They needed everything."

Many parts of the world started organizing huge relief efforts to Managua, and the idea of a similar effort from Puerto Rico was born, led by one of the island's most famous sons. Soon Clemente would be on a propeller-driven DC-7 stuffed with aid for the devastated country.

| CHAPTER TWO |

SACRIFICE

LUIS CLEMENTE: Sometimes, I just miss Dad being around. Not long ago, I was watching *61**, a film about New York Yankees players Roger Maris's and Mickey Mantle's attempts to break the single-season record of sixty home runs in a single season. Suddenly I broke into tears. I started crying with a lot of emotion. I went into the bathroom, washed my face, and looked into the mirror. I realized that's how I cried when I was a little kid. The feeling was for the first time in so many years, I was missing my dad so bad. I feel like every now and then my dad reaches out to me.

There was something else for me about that emotional day when I looked into the mirror. I realized that feeling of being a kid was never coming back. The truth is, I never got to be a kid. Roberto never got to be a kid. From the time our father died, we worked to continue his legacy. It's an honor to do that and something we cherish, but that's a true fact. We were never kids. We've never had our own lives. Ricky and I have stayed in Puerto Rico, while Roberto has spent most of his time in the States. Ricky has been afraid to fly after what happened to our dad.

The Clemente name in Puerto Rico is one of its greatest currencies, and the family protects it at all costs, even if they sacrifice a part of themselves to do so. This is not stated to get sympathy. I feel like this. My dad died a long time ago, and today buildings and streets are being named after him. I feel a personal responsibility to make sure he's protected.

You have to understand my dad to know how we are as a family. He was a very sincere person. If you asked him how he was doing, he thought you were sincere. He'd tell you, "You know, my back hurts; this hurts; that hurts." That sincerity was a big part of who he was, and it helped him care about people. He was very outspoken when it came to injustice—not just for any particular race, but for all people. So we all feel like we need to protect that. I know I say that a lot, but that's why we do what we do.

One day recently, I had a meeting with a Puerto Rican government official. Afterward, I stopped at a local bar, a place I'd been many times before, and upon entering was greeted warmly. There's one man in the bar who always says hello and I say hello back, but that was the extent of our past greetings. On this day, the man decided to say more than hi, and approached me. The man was slightly intoxicated, which may have been the reason for his sudden bluntness. "I gotta tell you, I observe you," he told me. "The first thing

you do is say hi to everyone. You are so nice, but I have to ask you, are you living your life? Because every time I hear you speak, it's about your father. I'm sorry to tell you, but your father's dead."

"THERE'S ALMOST A blank page in the lives of the sons when it comes to their father," says longtime family friend and confidant Chuck Berry, who has known the Clementes for decades. "They were never able to have that close relationship with their father because of the accident. They were left with the job of trying to live up to his legend.

"In my mind, if they sat down with a psychiatrist and talked about the pressures of growing up the son of Roberto Clemente, you'd see a lot of tears. They are such, in many ways, perfect kids. Compassionate, smart, and good-hearted, like their father. But imagine trying to live up to being their dad."

Both sons attempted baseball but could not be what their father was. Then

again, not many men in the history of the sport could. In June of 1986, then nineteen years old while playing for the Pittsburgh Pirates, his father's old franchise, Luis struggled. He had batted .235 the year before and worse that summer. The Pirates organization wanted to keep him in the system, but Luis knew it was over. "I wasn't going to be a token," he says now. "I'm going to bust my ass, but if you don't think I can play on the major-league level, then okay, but I'm not going to be a spectacle or a ticket.

"My son once asked me, 'Dad, what is the benefit of being Roberto Clemente's grandson? People expect so much from you,'" Luis says. "I tell him, 'You have to look at it the other way. You're very lucky. Your grandfather is still impacting so many people.'"

The Clemente family has also faced the same dilemma that's challenged many famous families: saying no.

"Sometimes I feel like telling people who try to take advantage of me to go screw themselves, but I can't," says Luis. "We can't. My mom won't let us. She doesn't ever want to hurt anyone. She never wants to say no. She makes other people's issues her issues."

Says Roberto: "I told Mom once, 'You have ruined me in some ways, because the word "no" isn't in my vocabulary.' We sometimes hurt ourselves because we don't say no."

VERA CLEMENTE: Roberto still impacts kids in Puerto Rico. They read about him in schoolbooks. They are taught that Roberto was a good person and they should try to be like him.

LUIS CLEMENTE: People still ask about my dad, what he was like, all these years later.

ROBERTO CLEMENTE JR.: There are schools around the country still being named after Dad.

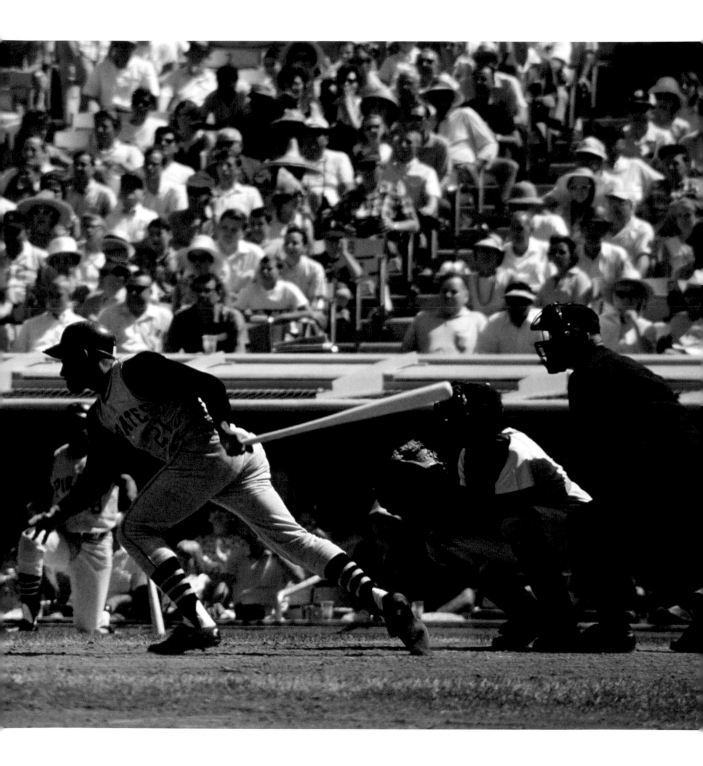

VERA CLEMENTE: There are people who come by the house asking about Roberto. It's been that way for a long time. After both of the World Series, our house would be full of strangers. Roberto welcomed everyone.

LUIS CLEMENTE: People will name their babies Roberto Clemente. They'll send the birth certificate to my mom asking her to sign it. She'll sign it with a nice note and send it back. They want Mom to sign it so they can fully explain to their son when he gets older why they named him after my dad.

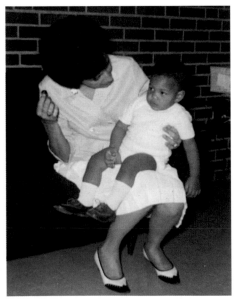

RICKY CLEMENTE: My dad was great, but my mom is incredible. Look at what she did. She raised us alone after our dad died. She never felt sorry for herself. She never abused the Clemente name. She's just a great person.

VERA CLEMENTE: Roberto would say, "I'll die young and not grow old. You'll probably remarry." I'd tell him, "Don't say things like that. Don't talk about sad things. God forbid something ever happened to you; I would never remarry."

ROBERTO CLEMENTE JR.: Mom took those words to Dad as a promise to him. No one would blame Mom if she remarried, but she was so dedicated to him.

LUIS CLEMENTE: Our mom is a saint. That's what you'll hear from everyone. She welcomes anyone into her home. She's nice to everyone. Dad used to tell her all the time he was going to die young. She'd say, "Stop talking like that." But he'd say it, and he'd tell Mom that if he did die young, she had to keep going on with her life. But Mom has been so loyal to Dad. She hasn't gone on so much as a lunch date.

I also think there's a small part of her that hopes someday, somehow, Dad will come back. He'll walk through the front door and be home again.

ROBERTO CLEMENTE JR.: I've had a different kind of challenge than some of my family members. I have the same name—Roberto—as my father. When I introduce myself to people who know the legacy of my father loosely, they recognize the name. When I meet people who know the Clemente name well and cherish it, they look at me intimately. To some, I am Clemente, and they act accordingly.

CLEMENTE

I was in Pittsburgh once and I stopped to assist a woman who had a flat tire. She was extremely grateful and began a conversation.

"Where are you from?" she asked me.

"I'm from Puerto Rico."

"Puerto Rico! That's where Roberto Clemente is from. He was such a great man. So what's your name?"

"Roberto Zabala." [He laughs.]

There are pictures of me in my diapers swinging a baseball bat. I was trying to be him. I played baseball in the major leagues like my dad. When I was eighteen, and at my first spring training with the Philadelphia Phillies in 1984, all I was ever asked was what it was like to be Roberto Clemente. People who knew my father would always

CLEMENTE

64

tell me how my father hit. "He could hit to right field. He could do this. He could do that." All I'd ever do was listen. I love my dad but I'm my own person.

Even at seven years old, following those terrible days after my dad died, I became him almost instantaneously. I was never personally able to mourn Dad's death. I was never able to cry. I was told, "You're the man of the house now. You have to be there for your mom." Literally, right after the accident, I went to school. In essence, I didn't really enjoy my childhood.

As the years went by, and everyone reminded me of how I looked like my father and acted like my father, each comment reminding me that my father was, in fact, gone, I thought of something drastic. I was thirteen. I went to my mom and said, "I want to change my name." She said, "It'll be okay. It'll be okay. It'll get better." There was so much pressure being Roberto Clemente, at that moment, I didn't want to be Roberto Clemente.

Then the sons again talk about their mother, and that word arises—sacrifice. It is clear the sons love and cherish their mother. Adore her, actually.

"The best thing my father did was pick the perfect wife and perfect mom for his kids," Roberto says.

"She rescued the family," says Luis.

Rescued?

"The family could have fallen apart after my father died," Luis says. "We could have fractured. She kept us together. She's a strong woman."

It is also clear to the sons that their mother is still deeply connected to their father.

"She still mourns him," says Roberto. "In essence, she's still married to my father."

CHAPTER THREE

MEMORIES

ROBERTO CLEMENTE JR.: In my mind, he is always floating.

TONY BARTIROME: He had these huge, strong hands. People always thought that because he hit with such power he was this big guy. He wasn't, especially by today's standards. He'd come into spring training at 185 pounds. At the end of the season, he was 181. The power came from those hands.

LUIS CLEMENTE: I remember when we were kids and we were playing with these toy guns with the suction cups. We were shooting them at a sliding glass door. It was getting late and we were loud. My dad slid back the door. He had these big hands. He grabbed our heads and said, "You're going to bed now."

ROBERTO CLEMENTE JR.: If I was doing something I wasn't supposed to be doing he'd just give me a look and I'd stop. He didn't have to say a word.

LUIS CLEMENTE: Ricky looks the most like our dad now. It's uncanny. Ricky is quiet but he's really funny. He jokes around a lot. He has Dad's respect for people. If he's driving, and there are cars headed to a funeral, he'll turn the radio off.

RICKY CLEMENTE: I was too young to truly get to know my dad, but I've learned everything about him. I try to treat people the way he treated people.

JUSTINO CLEMENTE WALKER: Roberto cared about people he didn't know. He also understood the impact he could have on people's lives. Just saying hello. Or going by hospitals to visit patients. He would go the funerals of strangers. He used to say, "I go to everyone else's funerals but maybe no one will come to mine."

LUIS CLEMENTE: Think about the irony of my dad wondering if people would go to his funeral. He never really got to have a funeral.

STEVE BLASS: Roberto could be serious, but people forget he could also be very, very funny. He was constantly cracking jokes. I went up to him one time and said, "If I ever get traded, and I face you, I'm going to pitch you inside." He said, "If you pitch me inside, I will hit the fucking ball to Harrisburg."

VERA CLEMENTE: There was an organ in the home that he would play. He'd play it with one finger. He'd drive while playing a [Hohner] harmonica.

LUIS CLEMENTE: My dad loved the U.S. and he was also very proud to be a Puerto Rican. He wanted each of his kids to be born in Puerto Rico. We all were.

ROBERTO CLEMENTE JR.: [Laughs.] He wanted me to play baseball but had some advice. . . . [He laughs again.] "Just don't play catcher. Their knees go bad."

THESE ARE THE memories of sons, Roberto's wife, and brother, and others. Roberto Jr. remembers waking, heading to breakfast, and in the kitchen would be a table full

74 CLEMENTE

of chicken, steak, and eggs. The blender would churn loudly as Clemente created a concoction of egg yolk, sugar, and orange or grapefruit juice, often his last meal before heading to the ballpark.

Roberto Jr. remembers his father watching scary movies late at night and sleeping through parts of the day—the latter being the life of a baseball player.

Strangers would knock on the door of the Clemente house in Puerto Rico. Clemente would answer, dressed in shorts and wearing no shirt, and he'd talk to people he didn't know, sometimes for hours. Some would come to the house in a wheelchair, or using crutches, or be in great pain. Clemente would work on their back or their legs the way a physical therapist does and the pain they'd arrived with would be gone when they left. Sometimes as a form of repayment, or simply out of adulation, people would leave gifts at the front door.

"One of the biggest memories I have was how I first realized just how big of a star he was, and that happened almost immediately after the accident," Roberto explains. "We came to our house and there were helicopters and police everywhere."

After the crash, on that beach where thousands came to hope and, eventually, to mourn, was Willie Montañez. Clemente had a profound effect on the life of Montañez almost a decade before the infamous flight. Montañez was a promising player in whom the Pirates had a great deal of interest. Just a matter of hours after the 1963 season ended, there was a knock on Montañez's door in Puerto

Los artistas y buenos peloteros Mome (el hijo de Melchor) y Pepe Pagán de visita en casa de Vitín Sánchez – Teaneck, N.J. Junio 28, 1969

Rico. "Hey, Willie," said Montañez's brother, "Roberto Clemente's here."

Clemente had come unannounced and with a message. He wanted Montañez to know that he was good enough to play in the major leagues, but there was another, equally important thing the young player had to digest. "You are a good player, good enough to play in the United States," Clemente said. "I do not think they are going to offer you the money you are worth. You can get more if you want to wait or maybe talk to other teams. Do not make the mistake of settling for less than you are worth."

MEMORIES . . . "HE IS standing on second base," Steve Blass, a pitcher for the Pirates, said of Clemente. "This is after he doubled off Jon Matlack for his three thousandth hit. He has one foot on the bag, and his hands are on his hips. The fans are cheering wildly, but he is just standing there, like a statue, the essence of dignity and pride and grace. That is my freeze-frame of him, how I picture him to this day."

"He never made a mistake in the field," remembered Joe Brown, who from 1956 to 1976 was the Pirates' general manager. "He

never threw to the wrong base, never failed to take the extra base, never was thrown out trying for the extra base. He was simply the most intelligent player who ever played for me."

"The size of his hands was exceeded only by the size of his heart," longtime friend Luis Mayoral once said. "One of my lasting memories of Roberto is also my last. Four days before he flew off to Nicaragua with relief supplies for the earthquake victims there, he was at Hiram Bithorn Stadium in San Juan, moving bags of goods, cartons of clothes. He could have just lent his name to the relief effort or done a public-service announcement. But there was Roberto, pardon the expression, working his ass off, and he had this look of determination. The same look he wore on the field at Three Rivers Stadium."

"Roberto was thoughtful and very quiet," remembered photographer Ozzie Sweet. "He'd answer questions, but he wasn't the type to initiate a conversation. He always had a serious expression, but when he held his hat over his heart, it became a special moment."

One story in a 1992 *Sports Illustrated* article on Clemente in many ways typified the star. Wrote the magazine: "Toward the end of his career he went into a store in Pitts-

burgh to buy ceramic supplies, only to have the proprietor refuse his money. 'Clemente, you won't remember this,' the man told him, 'but when I was a kid, ten or eleven years old, I was sitting in the right-field seats at Forbes Field while you were out there. I went for a foul ball, but an older man grabbed the ball away from me. I sat there, crying. The next inning you came over and said, "Here's a ball for the one they took away from you." I keep that ball in a place of honor in my home. That's why I can't charge you.'"

"In 1970 I was hitting three twenty-five in midseason," remembered Félix Milán, who played in Atlanta during Clemente's era, "and at dinner one night I told Roberto, 'I think I can hit three hundred this year.' He got mad. 'If you think you can hit three hundred,' he said, 'you will hit two eighty. If you think three twenty-five, then you will hit three hundred.' I did as he said and ended up hitting three ten."

Clemente was prideful and protective of the heritage of Latin ballplayers, which sometimes made him cautious, even defensive. By 1967, the Pirates had become a known commodity, and some of them, including Clemente, were asked to take small parts in a scene for the movie *The Odd Couple*. Clemente accepted the invitation, which came with a $100 payment. The script called for Clemente to hit into a double play. He went home and thought about it and by the next day was highly agitated about the prospect. Again, from *Sports Illustrated*: "The next day one of the producers came up to him and said, 'Hiya, Roberto. How's my old buddy?'

"'I am not old, I am not your buddy, and I am not going to be in your ——— movie,' Clemente said. 'How do you like that, old buddy?'

"Clemente then turned to a teammate and said, 'Nobody buys Roberto cheap. I have my pride. I am a hero to my people. Do they think Roberto Clemente was born

yesterday? Would they ask Cary Grant to play baseball for a hundred dollars? If fans in Puerto Rico see me hit into a triple play, they won't understand.' And that is why, in *The Odd Couple*, it is Bill Mazeroski who hits into the triple play."

This wasn't Clemente's ego talking. It was life experience—a life in which, while playing baseball in the United States, Clemente witnessed and experienced constant slights against the Latino player. More than slights: Clemente faced outright racism that turned a mild, kind man into a blunt and angry one. Also a confused one, since Clemente was raised to believe that the color of a person didn't matter. "I don't believe in color; I believe in people," Clemente said in one of the last interviews before his death. "I always respect everyone, and thanks to God my mother and my father taught me to never hate, never to dislike someone because of their color. I didn't even know about [racism] when I got [to Pittsburgh]."

Luisa Walker de Clemente, the mother of Roberto Clemente, who helped to in-

still many of Clemente's noble values, once shared her own memory of her son. "Roberto was born," she said, "to play baseball."

JUSTINO CLEMENTE WALKER: We did not grow up so poor as we are often portrayed. We were a [down-to-earth family]. None of the children were born in hospitals. We were all born in the house. We were all close.

LUIS CLEMENTE: My father didn't cart around milk bottles to generate money. That just didn't happen. That's become a huge myth.

VERA CLEMENTE: Roberto's parents worked hard. They were nice. They raised a good family.

JUSTINO CLEMENTE WALKER: We didn't have it as rough as our neighbors. We were the first house with a radio. Our friends would come over and listen to the shows on the radio. [He

CLEMENTE

laughs.] There were no milk bottles. The thing about Roberto is that he was a leader, and he was very passionate even at a young age.

When he was twelve, there was a car crash, and Roberto pulled a man from the wreckage of a car that was on fire.

At his school, there was no fence. People wanted a fence to help protect the school. He organized people to collect money to build the fence. He was eleven years old. If he was passionate about something, no one could con-

vince him otherwise, not even people in the family. That passion is why he had problems as a player in the U.S.

CLEMENTE USED TO joke that he got his strong throwing arm, the one that could seemingly throw people out from another star system, from his mother, Luisa. He was one of four athletic boys (seven children in total), and to keep them in line Luisa

developed formidable arm strength corralling her kids. Roberto Clemente was the youngest of sons born to Don Melchor Clemente and Luisa Walker on August 18, 1934, in Carolina. It should not come as a shock that the family was athletic. His brother Justino played amateur baseball, and some who saw him play say he was as talented as, if not more than, Roberto.

While Clemente had a strong work ethic, the long-repeated story that he awoke at sunrise, delivered heavy and clunky milk cans to neighborhood homes for thirty cents a month, and then went to school never happened. The story has been repeated in articles and books for so long it's come to be believed as fact. It fit a narrative comfortable with some who wanted to see Clemente as a poor, uneducated Puerto Rican child rescued from distinct poverty by American baseball.

In the book *Roberto Clemente*, written by United Press International writer Ira Miller almost immediately after Clemente's death, Miller spoke to Maria Isabel Caceres, who taught history at Julio Vizcarrondo High School in Carolina, Puerto Rico. Clemente would sit in the back of her class and rarely raise his hand. He was painfully shy as a kid. (Clemente would later pay for a surgery Caceres needed, and after becoming a Pirate he'd visit the high school every year after the baseball season. Clemente had planned to visit again shortly after his trip to Nicaragua. This was something almost no one knew at the time. Clemente never advertised it.)

While Clemente was shy in the classroom, on the baseball field—or any other field—he was dominant. An all-star for his high school baseball team for three consecutive years, he was also the best athlete on his track team, with the ability to high-

jump six feet, triple-jump forty-five feet, and throw the javelin 195 feet. Clemente would have likely made the Puerto Rican Olympic team and participated in the 1952 Olympics had it not been for baseball. The team could have used him—that year, no Puerto Rican athletes medaled in the games.

What made Clemente's abilities even more impressive compared to many of today's athletes was that he didn't use steroids or sophisticated training programs. His workouts, even as a professional player, consisted of running and moderate weight

CLEMENTE

lifting. The most anyone saw Clemente do was use ten-pound dumbbells or resistance bands to fine-tune his biceps.

Clemente kept a number of scrapbooks of his accomplishments before entering high school. Justino keeps them in his house in Carolina in a basement full of Clemente memorabilia. Roberto's handwritten notes appear throughout the books of photos and newspaper clippings. It is a remarkable thing to see, like Clemente speaking across the decades. One note, loosely translated, reads: "I loved the game so much that even though our playing field was muddy and we had many trees on it, I used to play many hours every day." Another: "The fences were about 150 feet away from home plate and I used to hit many homers. One day I hit ten home runs in a game we started about 11 a.m. and finished about 6:30 p.m."

The field where Clemente played high school baseball is now a stadium. It was renamed Roberto Clemente Stadium.

PIRATES TEAMMATE MANNY SANGUILLÉN: I don't know if people understand how athletic he was at an early age. He could do anything. He could run as fast as anybody.

JUSTINO CLEMENTE WALKER: Very few guys could outrun him when he was on the track team.

ROBERTO CLEMENTE JR.: Look at the pictures of him as a player. He's built like that, and it's all natural. He was a freak.

JUSTINO CLEMENTE WALKER: I went to all the games when Roberto played for Santurce. Once he was in the outfield and someone hit the ball over his head. I sank into my seat, embarrassed. He went chasing it, the ball bounced in front of the outfield wall, and he grabbed it off the ground. Then he put his foot against the wall, using it as leverage, and threw the runner out at third. I raised up in my seat after that.

At the age of eighteen, Clemente went to a park where Santurce was holding try-outs. The Crabbers would become one of baseball's hidden gems, producing dozens of major-league players. On this day, when Clemente went to the Crabbers, his battered and ripped glove in tow, the team allowed him to play shortstop. The owner of the Crabbers saw Clemente and was immediately impressed. Justino owns a copy of the contract that shows that for the 1952–1953 season, Clemente was to be paid $40 a week and a $500 bonus.

Player/manager Buster Clarkson knew that Clemente would be a great player, and it was Clarkson who kept pushing him to believe the same. Clemente told writer Ira Miller, "The fellow who helped me most of all is [Buster] Clarkson. Buck Clarkson used to tell me I am as good as anybody in the big leagues. That helped me a lot."

Clarkson said in an interview just prior to Clemente's death, "I could see he was going a long way. Some of the old-timers didn't think so, but I could see great ability in Clemente. He had a few rough spots, but he never made the same mistake twice."

This was a common description of Clemente throughout his career. Some would eventually call him one of the most studious and prepared players in baseball history, and it was this work ethic that allowed him to become almost flawless on defense and powerful on offense. Every spring training, long after his teammates would retreat to the clubhouse, Clemente would stay at the plate and swing at imaginary pitches. He practiced constantly in his mind. One afternoon, hours before the Pirates played the St. Louis Cardinals, Clemente was in the clubhouse, in a batting stance and raising his chin violently to the ceiling. Chin, ceiling. Chin, ceiling. A teammate noticed. "What are you doing?" he asked.

"We're facing Bob Gibson today," he said.

Gibson is one of the most talented pitchers baseball has ever seen. When he faced Clemente, he'd frequently throw several early pitches just under the chin of the Pittsburgh player.

"He had baseball savvy and listened," continued Clarkson about Clemente. "He listened to what he was told and he did it. . . . The main thing I had to do was keep his spirits up. He didn't realize how good he was. But I could see his potential. I had three good outfielders, but I had to give him a chance, and he broke into the regular lineup during the first season I managed Santurce. I always played him in right field and batted him first."

That first season with the Crabbers, Clemente hit .234 with eighteen hits in seventy-seven at-bats. In the outfield, he demonstrated sound judgment and skill. Clarkson, who besides managing the team was also a player, put Clemente in the outfield because of something more personal. Clemente's original position was shortstop, but that was where Clarkson played. If history had a taken an alternate course, baseball would be speaking of Clemente as one of the best shortstops of all time.

"Some of the old pros didn't take too kindly to a kid breaking into the lineup," Clarkson continued. "But Clemente was too good to keep out. . . . The big thing about Clemente was that he played hard and went all-out in every game. He did that when he was just a kid, and he did that all the way up through his last season. He always had that aggressiveness. I saw that from the first. Maybe it was the thing about him as a ballplayer that people will remember most.

"I told him," Clarkson explained, "he'd be as good as Willie Mays someday. And he was."

CHAPTER FOUR

"A Man of Honor Played Baseball Here"

LUIS CLEMENTE: We all loved baseball. All the kids. It's obvious why. It was in our blood. We played it from the time we were young. We tried to play with the same kind of passion and dedication my dad did. People always said that Roberto should be good because he was Roberto Clemente, or that I should be good because I was Luis Clemente. There were other things I loved to do, but it seemed like baseball was a natural.

I loved music, too. I played in a band in high school called Passage. We were pretty good. Two of the people in the band with me went to college to study music. I went to Florida to play baseball.

[Luis's music is reminiscent of some of the great rhythm-and-blues groups from the late 1980s and early 1990s.]

I was around the Pirates' clubhouse a lot growing up. After my dad died, all the Pirates players would look after us. We spent our summers around the Pirates. They were so good to us, and as I got older and kept playing baseball, they watched me and Roberto. When I was eighteen, the Pirates offered me a contract. I was following in my dad's footsteps. I was proud of that. I didn't want to be my dad. No one was that good. I wanted to honor my dad.

I didn't get along with the manager from the beginning [minor-league manager Woody Huyke from the Bradenton Pirates]. I got to training camp and the first time I met him he says to me, "So you're the little Clemente? While you're here, I'm going to make a man out of you. If you don't listen to me, you're going back to Puerto Rico." [Luis chuckles.] That was my welcome to the big leagues.

I tried hard. It just didn't work out. [He attempted a comeback several years later.] I had gotten a lot better, but I was in college in Puerto Rico and began to wonder if I was wasting time. I was going to go back to Puerto Rico and college. I asked to be released but they didn't want to do that. They thought that maybe I would get better and another club would want to sign me. They came to me and said, "Can you write a letter announcing your retirement and say thank you to us?" I said no.

I know from talking to my mom that my dad would have his battles with some of the managers and other people he played with early in his career. I think, because of

110 CLEMENTE

that, he initially didn't trust people easily. But he was very loyal. His old teammates always say, "Your dad was the best friend and teammate anyone could have." He had this way with his friends. He was very dedicated to them. If they needed money he helped them. If they needed a place to stay he helped. They were loyal to him and he returned that loyalty. [Luis and Roberto Jr. would demonstrate their own loyalty to their friends. Orlando Merced grew up several houses from the Clemente family and was six when Clemente died. The sons and Merced grew up friends, and later Luis and

PITTSBURGH		AVG	BALTIMORE		AVG
30 CASH	2B	289	6 BLAIR	CF	262
20 HEBNER	3B	271	7 BELANGER	SS	266
CLEMENTE	RF	341	14 RETTENMUND	LF	318
STARGELL	LF	295	20 ROBINSON	RF	281
16 OLIVER	CF	282	5 ROBINSON	3B	272
7 ROBERTSON	1B	271	26 POWELL	1B	256
35 SANGUILLEN	C	319	15 JOHNSON	2B	292
2 HERNANDEZ	SS	206	8 ETCHEBARREN	C	270
23 WALKER	P 10-8		37 DOBSON	P 20-8	

Roberto Jr. told the Pirates about Merced. Not long after that, the Pirates signed Merced. He'd go on to play thirteen years in the majors—six for the Pirates.]

My dad never asked for anything in return, and I think this is why his friends were so dedicated to him. When he died, you saw them repay that loyalty.

ONE DAY, MANNY Sanguillén would jump into an ocean, searching rugged waters for his friend. One day, he'd come to cherish Clemente. Love Clemente like a brother. He'd love him so much that he'd dive into the Atlantic Ocean looking for his friend in 120 feet of water, diving without any equipment as waves smashed his body. Birds circled overhead, and sharks could be seen not so far away. For eleven straight days, as President Richard Nixon expressed condolences, and a Puerto Rican people remained stunned, he canvassed part of an ocean alongside United States Navy divers. He looked in sand and blue water and canvassed a coral reef over fifty yards from shore. Five years earlier, in 1967, before he would honor his friend by searching for his body in the depths of an ocean, Manny Sanguillén would become one of Clemente's confidants, and that friendship would begin with yet another act of kindness from Clemente.

The first time they truly got to know each other was in Pittsburgh. Sanguillén was on the same flight with Clemente but didn't know it. Sanguillén was in the front portion of the plane and Clemente toward the rear. When Sanguillén disembarked, he noticed a crowd surrounding one of his fellow passengers, who had also just walked off the flight. The crowd started off with a few people asking the man for autographs. Then it grew to a few dozen, and within five minutes or so, the crowd had multiplied to more than fifty people. Sanguillén moved closer and saw that it was Clemente. He knew Clemente. Every Latin player at the very least knew of him. Heck, every baseball player did. Clemente signed autographs for more than an hour, and Sanguillén waited patiently.

Sanguillén introduced himself after the autograph seekers dispersed. "He welcomed me with open arms," said Sanguillén.

Sanguillén was headed to Forbes Field, while Clemente was headed elsewhere. Knowing that despite signing with a major-league team, the young player would be strapped for cash, Clemente paid for Sanguillén's taxi to the stadium.

"WE BECAME FRIENDS very quickly," Sanguillén says today. While telling the story, speaking of how he went to look for Clemente's body in the Atlantic Ocean after the plane crash, Sanguillén becomes emotional. People who speak about Clemente often do this. That's the effect he had on the lives of people who knew him well, and even some who did not.

After Clemente's death, Sanguillén, though a catcher, was asked to replace his close friend in right field. What's more, he was assigned to Clemente's old locker. The emotional strangeness of it all was too surreal for Sanguillén—his friend was gone, and here he was, playing his position and using his old locker. "I missed him so badly," Sanguillén said. "I still miss him."

Sanguillén and teammate Willie Stargell were at the Clemente home in Puerto Rico almost immediately after news of the accident broke. Sanguillén pulled Roberto Jr. aside and told him everything would be okay. "Your father is lost," Sanguillén told him, "and I'm going to try and find him."

The crash happened at a place called Punta Maldonado. It's a sliver of rock that juts out into the Atlantic from Piñones Beach (a visit there now shows there is no type of Clemente memorial at the scene). After the accident, the area was packed with hundreds of Puerto Rican people who waited for news as divers from the coast guard searched the waters for survivors and wreckage. On the first of eleven days, a rainbow hovered over the beach, and each day of those almost two weeks, hundreds came to the area, some hoping Clemente's body would be found. Others came to offer prayers and well-wishes.

Another Clemente teammate came to the beach in the aftermath of the accident besides Sanguillén. Blass went to San Juan almost immediately after news of the crash became public. He was stunned by what he saw. It was those hundreds of people, initially waiting for Clemente to return, then realizing he wouldn't, and then, paralyzed by this knowledge, waiting on the beach out of respect for as long as they could. "Those people didn't know what to do, so they went to the beach," he said. "Roberto was out there somewhere, so they went to the beach and waited."

Vera waited with them.

VERA CLEMENTE: For three months after the crash, I would receive a large package containing hundreds of letters from people around the world, expressing their

116 CLEMENTE

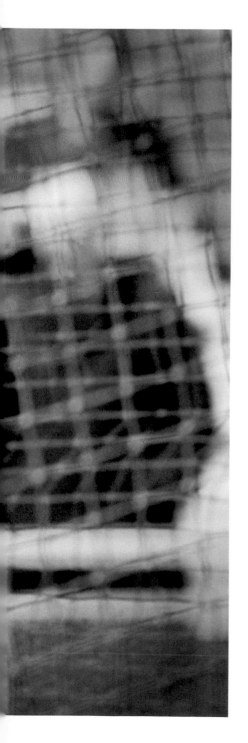

sorrow over my husband's death, and their well-wishes to me. The letters would keep coming, years later, especially at Christmas. I tried to answer as many as I could but there were too many.

Each afternoon, for weeks, I would go to that beach. I watched like everyone else. Once, there were fifty boats in the ocean, circling outside of the area where coast guard boats were searching. People in the boat tossed bouquets of flowers and wreaths into the water.

Then, one day, I stopped going.

I opened my home to well-wishers. That is part of Puerto Rican custom. Hundreds of people, in those days after the crash, paid their respects. The governor's office provided around-the-clock protection for the family but it wasn't truly needed. People were there to pay their respects, not harm us.

IF BABE RUTH or Hank Aaron or Branch Rickey or Rube Foster were nominees for the patriarch of baseball, Vera Clemente might be its matriarch. For decades Vera has presented the Roberto Clemente Award, given by Major League Baseball to the player who "best exemplifies the game of baseball, sportsmanship, community involvement, and the individual's contribution to his team." Vera is known throughout the sport. She can walk into almost any facility—from New York to Los Angeles—and people will know who she is and welcome her. Commissioner Bud Selig cherishes her, and

in Puerto Rico she is considered a national treasure. The steady undercurrent of that respect is that Vera has dedicated her life to carrying out her husband's wishes of being selfless. It was a mission started on that beach forty years ago.

In the 1974 biography of Clemente *Who Was Roberto?* writer Phil Musick described perfectly the immediate reaction to the loss of Clemente across the United States, Puerto Rico, and other parts of the world as news of the tragedy spread: "A resolution was introduced in the lower house of the legislature to rename the San Juan airport in honor of Clemente. A memorial fund was established to build Ciudad Deportiva [Sports City]. Children from a Brooklyn grade school pasted pennies to a sheet to form Clemente's uniform number, 21; the Pirates and a Pittsburgh foundation each donated a hundred thousand dollars to the Clemente fund. In a week the fund swelled to half a million dollars. After eulogizing the ballplayer, Richard Nixon called upon all Americans to donate. Throughout the island ecumenical masses were said . . . one day five little girls dressed in white released five white balloons that floated in the air above the flowers. A Pittsburgh congressman petitioned for a medallion to be struck in Clemente's memory, and a city park was renamed in his honor. The *Washington Post* editorialized: 'In Pittsburgh, at the empty Three Rivers Stadium yesterday, the scoreboard bore the legend, "Roberto Clemente, 1934–1972." It might have also read, "A man of honor played baseball here."'"

Said then governor-elect Rafael Hernández Colón: "Our people have lost one of their great glories."

Sanguillén remembers that time well, four decades later. When he is asked about it, his voice slows. "What everyone who knew Roberto will always remember first about him," says Sanguillén, "is that he had the biggest heart. He was a hero to me. I loved Roberto. He would do anything for you, and when he died, I had to go look for him, because I know he would have done the same for me."

"ONE OF THE things people ask me the most is 'How do I think my dad became such a great baseball player?'" says Roberto Jr. "When you talk to the guys he played with, they all say he worked hard. That was the thing. I can't tell you how many of his old teammates still say to me, 'Your father practiced and practiced and practiced.' He was like that from the time he was a kid. He was obsessed with the little things. He wanted to get things right, because he respected the game of baseball. He'd get to the ballpark very early and have guys hit the baseball to the corners of the stadium and practice how it bounced off the walls in the corners. He'd have all these ailments and fight through them. If he had

CLEMENTE

a bad back, he'd fight through it. He didn't want to let his teammates down, but he also had high standards for himself. You look at some of the players today with steroids and things." Roberto Jr. chuckles. "They didn't use steroids then. My father got strong just by being so active with baseball and trying to be a perfectionist."

IN A LATER era, the name Al Campanis would have different meaning. Campanis would go on television, speaking casually, as if he were sitting on his couch at

home, and talk of how blacks didn't have the necessities to become managers. Decades earlier, on a small baseball field in Puerto Rico, there had been no talk of prejudice regarding Campanis, no talk of bigotry, only talk of discovery.

In 1948, then working for the Brooklyn Dodgers, Campanis went to Santurce's Sixto Escobar Stadium. He wasn't optimistic. He watched some seventy young men

hitting and throwing, and none captured his attention until Clemente threw a ball toward home plate from deep center field. Campanis's eyes suddenly widened. He knew his time wasn't being wasted after all.

Campanis went into immediate scout mode. He tested Clemente in the sixty-yard dash, and the handheld stopwatch showed a blazing 6.4 seconds. It was one of the fastest times Campanis had ever seen. They moved to the batting cage, where Campanis would be even more impressed.

Campanis sent the other prospects home as Clemente began to hit. "Clemente got into the cage, and I noticed he stood far from the plate," Campanis was quoted as saying. "I had a minor-league pitcher there and I told him to keep the ball outside." That pitcher threw toward the edge of the plate, and Clemente hit every one.

"He hit line drives all over the place while I'm behind the cage telling myself we got to sign him if he can just hold that bat in his hands," Campanis added. "How could I miss him? He was the greatest natural athlete I ever saw as a free agent."

When Clemente signed with the Santurce Crabbers he was just seventeen years old. Years later, Campanis, despite the racist views he expressed in his television interview, kept three large photos on the wall of his Dodgers office of three men in particular whom he'd scouted and recruited: Sandy Koufax, Jackie Robinson, and Clemente. A Jewish man, a black man, and a Latino one.

CLEMENTE COULD BE temperamental, a trait that would last through much of his career. It was not unusual for him to threaten to quit if he didn't play more. What people from that time remember is a player far more mature than his age who was able to handle instruction and the competition from older players on the team. There was also Clemente's notorious work ethic. It was with Santurce that he truly

began to hone it. "Roberto could always handle pressure," says Sanguillén. "He had confidence. He wasn't intimidated by the older guys on the team."

As Clemente would reiterate throughout his life, it was Buster Clarkson who helped him the most in those days, and in typical Clemente form, he would never forget Clarkson's help. Later, as a Pittsburgh Pirate, he would speak highly of Clarkson to almost anyone who would listen. This was Clemente's way of paying Clarkson back. One of the things Clarkson did was stop Clemente from dragging his foot excessively as he activated his swing. Clemente remembered: "Clarkson put a bat behind my left foot to make sure I didn't drag it. He helped me as much as anyone. I was just a kid, but he insisted the older players let me take batting practice."

Clarkson said, "All he ever needed from me was encouragement. He had a few rough spots the first year, but he never made the same mistake twice, and he was always willing to listen."

Clarkson's words emphasize a critical point that needs to be remembered. Though born with great physical gifts, Clemente worked furiously to hone them. That trait is what distinguishes the good athlete from the eternal one.

On February 19, 1954, Clemente signed with the Dodgers and entered their minor-league system. One of the most important figures in baseball history was paid $5,000 for the season.

CHAPTER FIVE

HOMBRE INVISIBLE

LUIS CLEMENTE: All of the Clemente kids—Roberto, Ricky, and myself— have obviously spent so much of our lives in Puerto Rico. When you grow up in Puerto Rico, it's a very comfortable place. It's beautiful. There's lots of sun. There are beaches. Roberto Jr. has spent more time on the mainland than Ricky and me, but this is where he spent a good part of his life, too. You just get used to being here—the culture, the language, the pace of living. I can't imagine what it was like for my dad when he played in Canada. He didn't speak French. It was a very different place than where he grew up. It had to be tough because of the language, and he didn't know anyone. He was all alone in this foreign place.

JUSTINO CLEMENTE WALKER: The thing a lot of people don't know is that Tommy Lasorda played on that Montreal team. Lasorda really helped Roberto.

He helped Roberto the most with the language. Roberto was very grateful to him.

TOMMY LASORDA: He didn't know five words of English. I talked him out of quitting and going home to Puerto Rico three times. He was upset because he wasn't getting any playing time . . . the Dodgers tried to hide him. Scouts would show up and he was taken out of the game right away. I saw it happen in the first inning once.

VERA CLEMENTE: He was very, very lonely in Montreal.

MANNY SANGUILLÉN: [Laughs.] A Puerto Rican man in that cold weather is tough.

JUSTINO CLEMENTE WALKER: [The Dodgers] were hiding him. He did everything in Montreal—hit home runs, throw people out, run fast. He still didn't play. We talked one day and I asked him, "Why aren't they playing you?" He said, "I don't know. I feel uncomfortable here. I'm thinking about leaving here and never coming back."

JACKIE ROBINSON'S ENTRANCE into baseball was simultane-
ously historic, wonderful, and brutal. Clemente's entrance
was not so dissimilar, but was also more complicated. In
addition to racial differences, Clemente had the added bur-
den of a language barrier, and not just English. A man who
spent his life soaked in sun and Spanish went to the cold
and French of Canada.

Montreal in the 1950s was a place of electric streetcars,
modern architecture, and hockey riots. When a famous
Montreal Canadiens hockey player was suspended over a
controversial play, fans of the team rioted, leading to
$100,000 in property damage, more than a hundred ar-
rests, and some thirty-five people injured. Yet Montreal
welcomed Clemente. He lived with a white family in a
French part of the city. Teammate Joe Black remembers
the circumstances: "Montreal made blacks welcome
then," he once said. "The white family [Clemente] lived

with had two teenage daughters. That shows you how people treated us. Like we were human beings."

Clemente's brother Justino said that Clemente "wouldn't go out at night because of the racism when he first got to Montreal." A photo of Clemente's Montreal team shows three players of color.

"We had a lot of nuts on that team," Black also remembers. "They didn't appreciate a black guy who was a star. They only wanted you to go so far. But the guys on the team wondered why he wasn't playing. We had to scuffle, and when he played

the second games of doubleheaders, he seemed to make the difference. But we'd lose and they still wouldn't play him."

What happened in Montreal was immensely complicated and has been the subject of fervent historical debate by some baseball historians. In the end, there is little doubt that Clemente was hidden in the Dodgers' minor-league system so another club could not draft him in the off-season. The key was Clemente's salary and bonus, which totaled $15,000. At that time MLB teams, including Branch Rickey's Dodgers, started the practice of stockpiling talent in their minor-league systems as a way of

preventing other teams from making a play for them. It was both a brilliant and a diabolical practice. One year before Clemente signed his deal, baseball enacted a policy to counter that tactic. If a player signed for monies totaling more than $4,000 (that included salary and bonus), teams had to keep the player on the roster for two years or risk losing that player in the off-season draft.

The Dodgers attempted to hide Clemente in the baseball outpost that was the Montreal Royals, and play him so little that other teams wouldn't notice him. "This was a fact my dad really believed," says Roberto Jr.

It would seem impossible for a brown-skinned man who didn't speak French to be invisible in 1950s Canada, but that was almost the case with Clemente. His abilities were on display immediately, as he'd impress with his bat and glove despite sparse opportunities in Montreal, only to be sent back to the bench. In Clemente's

first week there, he hit a home run four hundred feet, sending it over a wall no Montreal hitter had ever cleared. In the next game, he was still benched. Clemente would get benched for a pinch hitter even with the bases loaded. In another game, he leaped so high over a left-field fence, snatching a ball out of the sky, his belt became stuck to the fence. While the Montreal team wouldn't play Clemente, he had nonetheless become a fan favorite. Canadians were fierce fans—of hockey—but still knew a star when they saw one. Spectators unclipped Clemente from the fence and applauded him.

Clemente hit a triple in another game and in the next was again benched. "The idea was to make me look bad," Clemente later said. "If I struck out, I stayed in there [the game]. If I played well, I was benched. Most of the season they used me as a pinch hitter or in second games of doubleheaders."

Dodgers general manager Buzzie Bavasi, in a first-person, rarely referenced story he wrote for the June 1967 *Sports Illustrated*, recalled: "We once owned Clemente. We signed him for a $10,000 bonus and sent him to Montreal for seasoning. He was a 19-year-old kid, right out of the winter leagues, and there wasn't any room for him on the roster of the big club. We ordered Montreal to keep him under wraps any way they could. Up there he was eligible for the baseball draft, and we didn't want to lose anybody as promising as this kid. On the other hand, we didn't realize how great he was or we'd have put him on the big club right away and protected him from the draft regardless of who we'd have to unload.

"At Montreal, to keep Clemente from looking too good, our manager, Max Macon, kept moving him in and out of the lineup. Poor Roberto! He'd strike out and

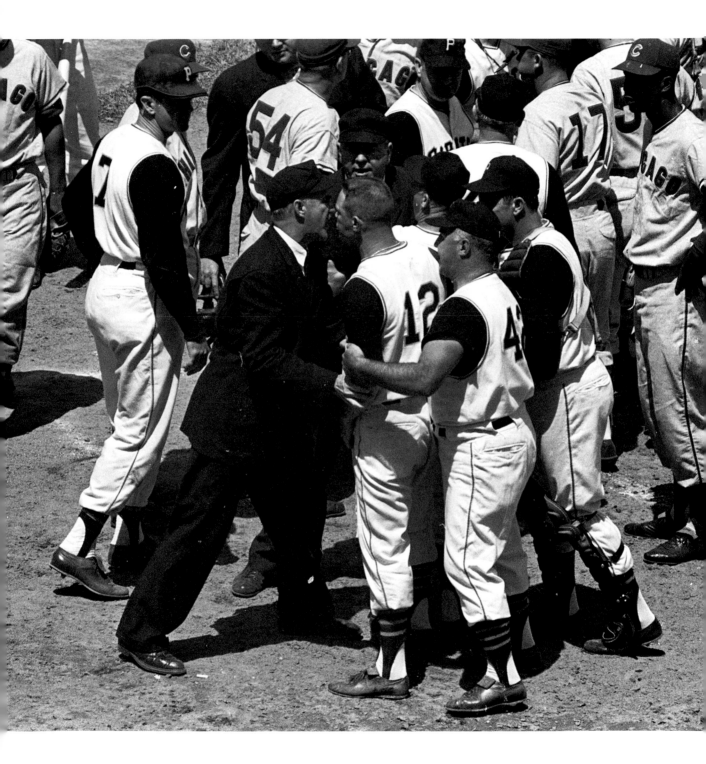

Max would let him play the whole game. If he hit a home run, Max would get him out of there quick. He was benched one game because he had hit three triples the day before. He was taken out for a pinch hitter with the bases loaded in the first inning of another game. You can imagine how this must have puzzled the kid. The net

effect was to hold his batting average down to .257, and we figured he was safe from the draft. But Clyde Sukeforth, who had come out of our own organization and now was scouting for the Pirates, had his eye on Roberto. He told Macon, 'Take good care of Clemente. We want him in good shape when we draft him.' "

Clemente learned a harsh lesson in Montreal that would stick with him throughout his career. Baseball was no longer just a sport he loved. It was a cold, nasty business. "I never thought I would reach such heights," Clemente said then. "Then I did . . . and they wouldn't let me play."

CLEMENTE WAS EXTREMELY intelligent, passionate, and friendly, but the early days of his career also made him cautious, as he progressed through baseball's maze of protocol and double standards. He began to evolve into a man who defended himself vigorously, after tiring of hearing what he couldn't do, when everyone who saw him play knew he was a multidimensional talent. The narrative of Clemente as a quiet and sort of strange hotdogging hypochondriac began appearing in the local

and national press. This, from an October 1960 *Sports Illustrated* article on the Pirates called "Seven Bold Bucs," about Clemente: "One of the most exciting of ballplayers, this trim, beautifully built athlete from Puerto Rico goes on batting rampages when no one can get him out. He swings viciously at any pitch within reach, loses his cap, runs through stop signs at third base, slides like an avalanche. Opposing ballplayers call him a hot-dog, say he can be intimidated by fast balls buzzing around his head—but pitchers have been throwing at him all year and he has hit .314, driven in almost 100 runs. Off the field Roberto is quiet, friendly, intelligent. Attended college briefly in Puerto Rico, where he threw the javelin. Something of a hypochondriac, Clemente once threatened to quit baseball because of an aching back, but has had few ailments this year. Only 26, he has been a big leaguer for six seasons, supports his father, mother, six other relatives."

Journalists at the time usually corrected the grammar of many white athletes, yet they often did not with Clemente and other Latin players. From the April 1961 *Sports Illustrated*: "'This is where it hurts. I had a very bad winter.' The speaker was Pirate Right Fielder Roberto Clemente, and he was pointing to his stomach, rubbing it gently. 'Something off with my diet. I eat the wrong food or too much food or not enough food. I don't know. Doctors don't know,' he said. 'I feel very bad at the World Series. That's why I did not do so well.' When reminded he hit .310 in the World Series, Clemente said: 'Yes, but I not hit with power.'"

Critics called him a hypochondriac, but his ailments—including lingering damage from his car accident—were real. The *New York Times* once listed every one from which he suffered. Backaches were the primary culprit, but there were bone chips in his right elbow, pulled muscles, a severely strained right instep, a thigh hematoma, tonsillitis, malaria, stomach issues, and perhaps most of all, insomnia.

"If I could sleep," he once told a teammate, "I would hit four hundred."

He sought relief from chiropractic medicine, which taught him to twist his neck and wrestle the vertebrae into place. Once, when asked how he felt, Clemente said, "Well, my bad shoulder feels good, but my good shoulder feels bad."

CHAPTER SIX

EMERGENCE

ROBERTO CLEMENTE JR.: My mom always says, "Your dad was a proud man. He stood up for himself." Sometimes I think people may have interpreted that the wrong way. He wanted to set a good example for the Latin ballplayer. I think he wanted people to know that they were as talented as anyone else. I think Dad felt like he had to constantly prove himself.

ROBERTO CLEMENTE, 1961, AFTER WINNING THE SILVER BAT FOR BEING THE LEAGUE'S BEST HITTER: In the name of my family, in the name of Puerto Rico, in the name of all the players who didn't have a chance to play for Puerto Rico in the big leagues, I thank you. You can be sure that all the Puerto Rican players who go the States do their best.

CLEMENTE WAS MANY things to many people. Most of all, he was a good man. He was not, however, a flawless man. His pride was like a type of shield that enabled him to

endure the various indignities of the time. From a January 1973 *Sports Illustrated*, which appeared shortly after Clemente's death: "When Roberto Clemente was breaking into the major leagues with the Pittsburgh Pirates in 1955, Henry Aaron had already established himself as a star and Willie Mays had won a batting championship, had been named Most Valuable Player, had helped his team win two pennants and the autumn before had made one of the most spectacular catches in World Series history. Clemente was having a modest rookie season: a .255 batting average, only five home runs, only

47 runs batted in. Yet the extraordinary skills were already evident, and one day that season in New York the 21-year-old Clemente was invited to appear on a postgame interview. The announcer reviewed his playing and then, thinking to give the youngster a compliment he could savor, said, 'Roberto, you had a fine day and a fine series here. As a young fellow starting out you remind me of another rookie outfielder who could run, throw and get those clutch hits. Young fellow of ours, name of Willie Mays.' There was a noticeable silence. Then the Pittsburgh rookie answered, 'Nonetheless, I play like Roberto Clemente.'

"Such pride, such insistence that he be respected for what he was himself, was the hallmark of Roberto Clemente."

Before playing the Orioles, Clemente declared that "nobody does anything better than me in baseball." It wasn't said with arrogance but in defiance of those in the

CLEMENTE

media who had mocked him personally and derided his abilities and those of other Puerto Rican baseball players.

As Clemente's talents became more recognized, some in the media, as well as Topps baseball card company, attempted to de-Latino Clemente by referring to him as "Bob." He refused to accept the name. He repeatedly insisted he be called Roberto.

That same pride sometimes caused Clemente to be overly defensive.

One of the greater moments of frustration for Clemente came while he was in Montreal. Clemente was scheduled to bat seventh against a pitcher named Jackie Collum. When Collum was four years old, the middle and index fingers on his left hand were severed after being caught in a piece of farm machinery. Thus, Collum had difficulty throwing a fastball, and relied on throwing sliders and off-speed pitches.

In the first inning, Montreal hitters blasted Collum, and then, batting seventh, it was Clemente's turn. He headed out of the dugout, but before reaching the batter's box, Clemente was pulled back by manager Max Macon, and replaced. That moment was one of the more indicative of how the Dodgers were indeed burying Clemente to keep him from prospering, and Clemente had seen enough. He was furious.

Clemente went back to his hotel and began packing to leave when there was a knock at the door. It was Pirates scout Howard Haak. He'd been assigned to watch Clemente and, like almost everyone who saw him play, was stunned at his abilities. Haak knew that Clemente could help transform the fortunes of the Pirates almost immediately. Haak

reminded Clemente that leaving would contractually bind him to playing for the Dodgers. But if he stayed, the Pirates would draft him. Clemente calmed himself, stopped packing, and listened intently. His intellect took over and his passions cooled. "Finish the year," Haak told Clemente, "and next season you'll be playing every day for the Pirates."

ROBERTO CLEMENTE JR.: Dad obviously had a lot of respect for Willie Mays. When some of Dad's teammates talk about [Mays], they always thought Dad respected him highly but was also really competitive with him. I think Dad thought Willie was respected, while Dad felt like he had to fight for respect.

CLEMENTE AND MAYS would each earn twelve Gold Glove awards, a record for outfielders. While Mays would become the bigger name, he wasn't the greater talent. In preparation for this first season with the Pirates, Clemente returned to Santurce, and

while his first year at Santurce had been frustrating at times, his second time was vastly different. It was on this second go-round that Clemente truly started to open eyes, mainly because he was playing next to Mays. Mays was four years older than Clemente, and the younger player was watchful, studious, and respectful. "Don't let the pitchers here show you up," Mays would tell Clemente. "Get mean when you go to bat. If they try to knock you down, act like it doesn't bother you. Get up and hit the ball. Show them."

It was the winter of 1954, and Clemente would use his time around Mays to hone not just his baseball skills but his competitive drive. Clemente would be ready for the major leagues, but a man who spent his life in Puerto Rico wasn't ready for Pittsburgh. Clemente told one writer at the time, "I didn't even know where Pittsburgh was."

The climate and culture were, of course, dramatically different. Pittsburgh was at the beginning of a renaissance that saw the city transform itself from a smog pit with polluted rivers to a cleaner place. Like many other American cities at the time, Pittsburgh was highly segregated, with African-Americans predominantly living in an area called the Hill District. "I couldn't speak English," Clemente remembered. "Not to speak the language . . . that is a terrible problem. Not to speak the language meant you were different."

"He was a rare individual, and by that I don't mean strange," says Bill Virdon, the only man to play with, coach, and manage Clemente. "He was a stranger from another country, and he didn't understand our ways. We didn't understand his ways. The first two or three years he was in Pittsburgh, we kind of frowned on some of the things he did. We thought there was something wrong with him when he didn't play sometimes, but as we learned more about each other, we really learned to appreciate him. All the years I managed, I never managed a more cooperative and understanding player."

JUSTINO CLEMENTE: The Pirates drafted Clemente and they got him for $4,000. It's the greatest bargain in baseball history. [Laughs.]

VERA CLEMENTE: What confused my husband most, I think, when he came to [the United States] was [the looseness of] the language. In Puerto Rico, we say what we think. This is how we were all raised. We're direct. If we ask, "How are you?" We mean, "How are you?" We want to know the answer. [Roberto] would say, "If you really don't want to know how I'm feeling, then why ask me?"

"I REMEMBER HIM driving us around Puerto Rico a few weeks before he died," said the late former Pirates pitcher and broadcaster Nellie King. "He was so proud of the place. And he said, 'I tell you something about Puerto Rico. When they love you here, they give you the shirt off their backs. But if they tell you, "If you come around here tomorrow, I'm going to kill you," that means that if you come around that place tomorrow, they are going to kill you.'"

In many ways, as strange as it seems, Clemente's sincerity, his directness, was off-putting to some. The fact that Clemente despised pretentiousness should have been an endearing quality, but initially it added to the narrative that he was different. While many Pittsburgh fans and teammates showed Clemente great respect, others behaved with remarkable insensitivity. A woman fan once asked Clemente whether he wore a loincloth when living in Puerto Rico.

In the late 1950s, Clemente was one of about two dozen Latin players in the major

leagues. There were two Latinos on the Pirates in 1955. Some sportswriters didn't even bother to hide their disdain. One wrote that Clemente was the "chocolate-colored islander." When Clemente would say he hit the ball they would spell "hit" "heet."

"No, me no married yet," one newspaper quoted Clemente as saying, "not even girl. I still too yong. Plenty time. I make beeg ligues first." If Clemente hit a homer, he'd be ignored by some of the journalists. They'd talk to other players instead. Unable to digest the fact that Clemente was an outstanding athlete, they called him a hot dog. Specifically, one writer called him a Puerto Rican hot dog. If he didn't play because he was injured, he was called lazy.

Clemente represented a swath of players after Jackie Robinson who made it into baseball but, because of the color of their skin, still faced terrible racism. These weren't just black players but also Latin players and various mixes thereof. They had to deal with the sting of prejudice while also facing the thorniness of a language barrier. Baseball executives and managers did little or nothing to prepare these players for the world they were entering. Clemente wasn't just brave in staring down the bigotry he faced; he also took on white teammates who were hateful to Pirates of color. The first black player in the history of the Pittsburgh franchise was second baseman Curt Roberts. Clemente said in an interview with United Press International writer Milton Richman, "I didn't like some of the things the white players said to Roberts, so I said some things to them they didn't like."

This is the baseball world Clemente entered.

VERA CLEMENTE: My husband was never scared to talk about civil rights. He watched the civil rights battles in the South and felt very close to them. He met Martin Luther King several times. Roberto wanted to do his part for baseball, so he would speak out about the issues in baseball. He'd talk a lot about how being a black Latino coming into baseball meant you had two strikes against you. He wanted the Latino players to get their fair share of money. He wanted them to be managers. Roberto was very vocal. The biggest thing he wanted was the Latin player to get his respect.

SLOWLY, AMERICA WAS beginning to fully digest Clemente as both a player and a human being. The country liked what it saw. Most did, anyway. On September 29, 1972, at the

start of a series between the Pirates and the New York Mets, a man sent a typewritten note in red ink to Three Rivers Stadium. The letter began simply: "To Mr. Roberto Clemente."

The letter continued: "ON SEPTEMBER 29TH, FRIDAY AT PITTSBURGH PIRATES THREE RIVERS STADIUM IN THE TOP OF THE SECOND INNING YOU WILL BE SHOT WHILE PLAYING RIGHT FIELD. I'LL BE WAITING FOR YOU. LET'S SAY IT'S A PRESENT FROM A METS FAN. SEE YOU IN HELL. P.S. DID YOU EVER GET SHOT WITH A SHOTGUN BEFORE?"

The letter was sent to the Pirates as regular fan mail but wasn't discovered by the Pirates until November 1. The team notified the FBI. According to the FBI's own files, the agency took the threat seriously, with its laboratories testing the note for foren-

sic evidence but finding none. Clemente at the time was in San Juan, and the FBI contacted him there to warn him about the threat. The author of the letter was never identified and the FBI closed its investigation.

IN HIS EARLY days with the Pirates, Clemente would hear the racial slurs and try to ignore them. Some of his teammates would yell them at opposing black players. Clemente would hear racial slurs, become disgusted, and move to the opposite side of the dugout. "Sometimes I acted like I didn't hear it," he once said. "But I heard it. I heard it."

Other times, Clemente would confront his teammates directly. After the assassination of Martin Luther King, players took a poll on whether they should play that night. "If you have to ask," Clemente would say of the meeting, "we do not have a great country."

Clemente pushed Pirates management to sign more players of color, and they listened. When Clemente went to the Pirates in 1955, the team was a collection of white men. By the early 1970s, approximately half of the Pirate roster was either black, Latin, or spoke Spanish.

His first major-league hit came in 1955 against the Brooklyn team (and farm system) that had shunned him. Clemente singled a pitch from Johnny Podres, and just like that his career began. That moment signaled something else: Clemente was physically strong, but no hitter could muscle Forbes Field. It was a monstrosity—457 feet to left-center field. Clemente knew he wasn't capable of beating Forbes with his biceps, so he used brains and finesse. He became a singles hitter.

It was an interesting time for both the country and Clemente. Outside of the clubhouse, he studied the news of what was happening in the South. He followed Rosa Parks's civil disobedience and the murder of fourteen-year-old Emmett Till in Mississippi for flirting with a white woman. Clemente wasn't fighting for his life or the freedom of an entire race, but he was fighting nonetheless.

Clemente was an oddity in the Pittsburgh clubhouse, not solely because of his ethnicity and how he spoke, but also for how he approached his craft. Clemente's grumpy back kept him out of the lineup on occasion, and this caused some of Clemente's teammates to not just mock his injuries but question his toughness and dedication. Pirates pitcher Nellie King told writer Phil Musick in 1973, "[N]o one then seemed to realize the sensitivity he had for his body. He looked at it the way a mechanic looks at a racing car. If he wasn't right, he wanted to tune it. Some guys used to ridicule him because he didn't play every day, but most of them were playing every day so people would say, 'Gee, that guy has balls.' They were doing it because they were afraid of criticism if they didn't. The only thing that dictated what Clemente did was what he felt was right. . . . I know Roberto was hurt deeply by the criticism he

took the first years [in Pittsburgh]. He was withdrawn partly because of the language. He'd only ever been out of Puerto Rico one other time. Everything [in Pittsburgh] was confusing to him."

Some two decades later, King would give perhaps the best quote ever regarding Clemente's creative skills and views about his body. King told the *Sporting News* in 1992, "I always looked at him as an artist, and artistic people have sensitivities that the rest of us don't have. We think they're crazy. His special sensitivity was to his body. 'People who pay to see me perform pay to see me at my best,' he would say. He told us once, 'In the summer, I play baseball. In the winter, I work baseball. In the summer, when I get hurt playing, I write down what I hurt, the date I hurt it, and how I hurt it. In the winter, I look at that chart, and I see where my body is weak, and I work to strengthen that part of my body.'"

CHAPTER SEVEN

PREMONITIONS

ROBERTO CLEMENTE JR.: I was seven years old, in my bed, trying to sleep. I woke up from a dream, but it was more. It was a vision. My father was going to die. I climbed out of bed and ran to my dad.

He was catching a flight the next morning. "The plane is going to crash," I told him. My dad rarely slept during the early morning hours, himself an occasional victim of insomnia. In some of my father's own dreams, he was on a plane, spiraling downward. He would tell my mom, Vera, "I'm going to die young."

My words caused my dad to sit up.

"Don't go on the plane," I told my dad.

"Why?" he said.

"The plane is going to crash."

"It's okay," my dad said. "Go back to sleep."

VERA CLEMENTE: AFTER my husband died, I did wait for him. I was hoping he'd come home. This went on for years. I kept his clothes in the closet. His drawers still had his clothes. This went on for a long time. Then one morning I saw Ricky sitting in front of the television. Ricky was five at the time. He was too young to really know his father. He was watching an old film about Roberto. In the film, Roberto was playing baseball with some children. Right next to Ricky, close to him on the floor, were some of Roberto's clothes he had taken out of the drawer. It broke my heart. I put all of Roberto's clothes that were in the closet and drawers away after that.

One day, a little less than a month after the accident, I couldn't find Roberto Jr. in the house. I looked all over. I found him in a back part of the house. He had gathered all of the newspaper clippings about his dad and was looking over them.

Roberto Jr. always wanted to be like his father. I remember, not long after the crash, it was bedtime for him, and we were talking. "Mommy, tell the Pirates not to put anyone in right field," he told me. "I want to play the right field for the Pirates."

I told him one day it could happen. "No, Mommy," he told me, "I want to play right now."

C<small>LEMENTE AND</small> R<small>OBERTO</small> Jr. weren't the
only ones who had premonitions about
that flight. Not long before that, Pirates
teammate José Pagán questioned the
safety of the aircraft. "You know everything about baseball," Pagán said. "But
you know nothing about airplanes."

Clemente was trusting of the pilot.
"The people in charge know what they're
doing," he told Pagán. "They will not let
us take off if we can't make it. If you are
supposed to die, you are going to die."

Just one of the five bodies aboard the
plane was recovered. Clemente's was not
the one. The Federal Aviation Adminis-
tration returned to Vera a suitcase that
belonged to her husband. Inside was
$1,000 in cash and a list of names believed
to be Nicaraguan citizens. Clemente, in
addition to galvanizing support in
Puerto Rico that led to the donation of
tons of supplies in about six days, had
also told a number of Nicaraguans he
would help discover whether relatives
and friends had survived the earthquake.
Thus, the list of names. Rescuers also
found a brown sock. Vera knew it belonged to her husband.

THE PREMONITIONS HAVE always given Clemente's legacy an almost spiritual, if not devotional, feel. Jon Matlack, a former pitcher for the New York Mets, met Clemente while Matlack was a teenager playing winter baseball in San Juan. Clemente invited Matlack and a group of other young players to his house. At that point, Clemente had already been a multiple All-Star. Matlack was awestruck, and not just because he was in Clemente's presence, but because Clemente had welcomed Matlack into his home. Young players weren't used to stars being so hospitable. Clemente laughed and joked with the group like he had known them for years. Then Matlack noticed something. His attention was drawn to the bat Clemente was holding. It was mas-

sive, and Clemente's large hands tossed it around as if he were holding a cigar. Matlack thought it looked like a club. He became so fixated on the bat that he went to pick it up when Clemente had put it on the floor to leave the room for a moment. When Matlack picked up the bat, he was impressed at its heavy weight.

He also thought: *Any man who can swing a bat like this is going to make history.*

Matlack would find out himself years later, when his curveball was drilled to left-center for Clemente's record-setting three thousandth hit.

ROBERTO CLEMENTE JR.: Everything my dad was about, how he dedicated his life to helping others, is summed up, in a way, with how he died.

VERA CLEMENTE: He would go down the street to help someone or go around the world. Whenever we traveled, he would leave the hotel to meet the real people. He would walk the streets and look for the common person. He never forgot what it was like for him growing up in Puerto Rico. When he played for the Pirates, whenever they traveled, he would visit kids in a hospital.

We went to Nicaragua [Clemente was managing the Puerto Rican amateur baseball team that traveled to Nicaragua for the Amateur Baseball World Series], and while there Roberto and other Pirates players visited [El Retiro hospital]. He met a lot of people. One was a little boy [twelve-year-old Julio Parrales] who could not walk because of an accident. [He was wheelchair-bound after, while playing on some railroad tracks, he lost one of his legs and had the other severely injured.] Roberto really liked him. He told the boy, "I'm going to help you." Roberto donated the prosthetic legs to Parrales so that he could walk again.

He felt a closeness to Nicaragua, because he met so many people who were poor and needed help.

LUIS CLEMENTE: After the earthquake you had entire countries organizing relief efforts. In Puerto Rico, it was basically Mom, Dad, some civic leaders and artists. But mostly it was Mom and Dad. It was the only time Dad really used the Clemente name.

[The boy who had such a profound impact on Clemente died in the earthquake. Clemente never knew about the boy's death.]

VERA CLEMENTE: One afternoon, Roberto went on TV, channel four in Puerto Rico, to ask people to donate. So many things came in—food, clothes, and medicine. It was incredible. People in Nicaragua were telling us specifically what they needed. We were communicating by CB radio. [Two collection places for the aid were set up—at Hiram Bithorn Stadium and the Plaza Las Américas.]

Flights started to go over with aid. The first flight had five X-ray machines. There was also a freighter. Not many people remember that there was a

freighter. [It carried 210 tons of clothing and thirty-six tons of food.] Puerto Rico raised over $150,000 in money and aid.

LUIS CLEMENTE: The rumor that's lasted all this time is that he went to Managua because he had a girlfriend there. It's just not true.

VERA CLEMENTE: [Laughing.] There was no girlfriend. I was with him all the time. He was a se-

rious and formal man and dedicated to his family. That rumor comes from the fact that we were going to bring back [a nanny] who could help with the kids.

The first three flights were on regular cargo planes. The fourth flight was in a DC-7 cargo plane, the one that crashed. The day before the accident, we sent a boat loaded with supplies.

Two weeks before the accident, there was a picture in the local newspaper of the plane, saying it was having problems. I didn't know about that picture until after the accident happened.

LUIS CLEMENTE: There were so many strange things from that flight and that day.

JUSTINO CLEMENTE WALKER: Roberto saw the plane just a little while before they were going to leave and noticed the tires. He said, "The tires look kind of low."

VERA CLEMENTE: I was making lunch for us [her and Roberto] before the flight. Roberto was trying to sleep to get ready for the flight to Nicaragua. I was in the kitchen and there was a song playing in my head over and over. [It was *"Tragedia de Viernes Santo,"* a highly popular song about a DC-4 that crashed into the ocean after departing San Juan for New York on Good Friday in 1952.]

LUIS CLEMENTE: I think Dad was having this inner fight. He felt like something may have been wrong with the plane, and didn't want to get on, but he also thought, "I have to go. I have to make sure everything's okay in Nicaragua."

VERA CLEMENTE: He was also going to bring back five friends who were in Nicaragua working as volunteers at the Maseya hospital. When the plane took off, the water was rough, and it started to rain.

I got a call about the accident. I didn't accept it. I said no.

JUSTINO CLEMENTE WALKER: The divers pulled a body out of the water. It was put on a helicopter. The crowd at the beach was really large, hundreds of people. The helicopter moved slowly overhead toward where it was going to

land. The crowd of people thought the body was Roberto's. Everyone ran, following the helicopter, but the body was the pilot.

PIRATES TEAMMATE WILLIE STARGELL, AT CLEMENTE'S MEMORIAL SERVICE: I'll tell you, it's really hard to put into words all the feelings that I have for Roberto. Since I've been with him I've had a chance to know a really

dynamic man who walked tall in every sense you can think of. He was proud; he was dedicated. He was in every sense you can determine a man. And I think going the way he went really typifies how he lived. Helping other people without seeking any publicity or fame. Just making sure that he could lend a hand and get the job done . . . The greatness that he is, we all know the ballplayer that he is. For those that did not know him as a man, they really missed a fine treat for not knowing this gentleman. I had the opportunity to play with him, to sit down and talk about the things that friends talk about. And I am losing a great friend. But he will always remain in my heart.

RICHARD NIXON IN WHITE HOUSE STATEMENT: The best memorial we can build to his memory is to contribute generously for the relief of those he was trying to help—the earthquake victims in Nicaragua.

PUERTO RICAN WRITER ELLIOTT CASTRO: That night on which Roberto Clemente left us physically, his immortality began.

LUIS CLEMENTE: My dad was obsessed with the number three. He'd have visions of his sister who had died, appearing to him, holding three gold coins. Three thousand hits . . . his uniform number, 21 . . ."

VERA CLEMENTE: A few days after the crash, Roberto Jr. would pick up the phone and pretend he was talking to his father.

ROBERTO CLEMENTE JR.: The night of the premonition . . . the night before that flight . . . the night I went to my father and told him not to fly and

he told me, "Roberto, it will be okay" . . . all these decades later . . . I remember. There are pangs of guilt.

In the days after my dad's death, as millions of people from Puerto Rico to Pittsburgh to Nicaragua realized that my dad was indeed never coming back, photographers snapped me kissing a poster that held a picture of my father. That image was as emotional to Puerto Ricans as the picture of John F. Kennedy Jr. saluting the coffin of his assassinated father.

Now, remembering those memories today, it's the fortieth anniversary of my father's death. For me, the week prior was probably tougher. The day of

the anniversary, I had been readying myself. I braced myself. I knew what was coming. The week before is when my emotions start flying. Every other part of the year, I'm fine. I speak to students and we talk about my father. I speak to young kids about my father and I'm okay. People ask questions about him, talk to me about him, and everything is fine. It's the one time of the year when things get tough and I have these feelings of guilt. I feel like I could

have stopped him. I went to him about my dream. I tried to tell him, but I was so young. I didn't have all of the words to explain everything fully. If I was able to better explain about the vision I had, he would have never gotten on that plane. If I could have told him more directly, I could have saved my father's life.

CHAPTER EIGHT

ETERNAL

Just before the 1971 season, Clemente yet again demonstrated his ability to move people deeply. Standing before national media gathered for the annual Baseball Writers' Association of America banquet in Houston, he was presented the Tris Speaker award, given for lifetime achievement in the sport of baseball. After his acceptance speech, Clemente received a standing ovation from more than eight hundred hardened, cynical baseball writers. It was this thought Clemente expressed that caused some eyes in the room to water:

"If you have a chance to accomplish something that will make things better for people coming behind you, and you don't do that, you are wasting your time on this Earth."

Clemente added that people should "live together and work together, no matter what race or nationality."

VERA CLEMENTE: He felt very comfortable with that 1971 Pirates team. He didn't feel alone.

ROBERTO CLEMENTE JR.: That team represented America. It really did.

[The Pirates in 1971 fielded the first all-black-and-Latino lineup in major-league history. It lasted one inning, because one of the players, pitcher Dock Ellis, was taken out of the game after giving up four runs in the second inning.]

STEVE BLASS: [Speaking of diversity of leadership.] You had a Latino player in Clemente, a black guy [in] Willie Stargell, and a white guy in Bill Maze-roski. We had the whole program covered. They were leaders—all three of them. . . .

TONY BARTIROME: He had experienced a lot of racism and never became bitter. If you saw the conditions the black players had to live in [during spring training in the late 1950s], you would have been shocked. They had to live there because racism prevented them from living in the better places with the white players. He fought to make things in baseball equal.

LUIS CLEMENTE: Dad was proud he was able to help diversify that team. You saw that pride when he spoke on the night dedicated to him.

ROBERTO CLEMENTE, ON ROBERTO CLEMENTE NIGHT AT THREE RIVERS STADIUM: I would like to dedicate this honor to all the Puerto Rican mothers. I don't have words to express this thankfulness. I only ask those who are watching this program and are close to their parents, ask for their blessing, and that they have each other. As those friends who are watching this program or listening to it on the radio shake each other's hands as a sign of friendship that united all of us Puerto Ricans. I've sacrificed these sixteen

years, maybe I've lost many friendships due to the effort it takes for someone to try to do the maximum in sports and especially the work it takes for us, the Puerto Ricans, especially for the Latinos, to triumph in the big leagues. I have achieved this triumph for us, the Latinos. I believe that it is a matter of pride for all of us, the Puerto Ricans as well as those in the Caribbean, because we are all brothers. . . .

CLEMENTE WAS, WELL, Clemente in the World Series against Baltimore. The first two games typified how he played whenever appearing in a huge moment. In the first two games, he had four hits in nine at-bats, and also made the play of the World Series. It was the kind of play he had made in Puerto Rico as a kid, in Montreal as a frustrated, budding star, and so many times as a Pirate.

In the second game, Merv Rettenmund, one of Baltimore's fastest players, was on second base. A ball was hit deep toward Clemente, down the right-field line, and it seemed a simple matter that Rettenmund would advance to third base. Clemente chased down the ball while at full gallop and caught it, his inertia still pulling him forward. Amazingly, Clemente stopped himself, pivoted, and made a one-hop, three-hundred-foot throw to third, which turned a routine tag by Rettenmund into a fight for survival. Rettenmund slid into third and was barely ruled safe.

Orioles catcher Andy Etchebarren, whose career lasted from 1962 to 1978, told sportswriter Dick Young the throw was the greatest he had ever seen by an outfielder.

VERA CLEMENTE: The night before Game 1 of the World Series, we were in Maryland. Roberto and I went to a seafood restaurant. Roberto had clams and got really sick. He had food poisoning. He was throwing up. The team

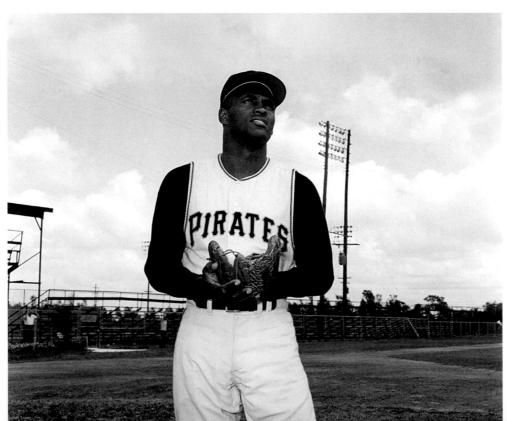

doctor was worried and I was really worried. He had to get fluids intravenously in our hotel room [at the Lord Baltimore Hotel]. We didn't sleep at all. I wasn't sure he was going to be able to play but he did. Then he goes into the game and still plays well. Almost no one knew how sick he was. [Clemente had two hits in the game—a double in the first inning and a single to center in the second.] He was so determined.

MANNY SANGUILLÉN: He played like a champion in that World Series. The world got to see how great he was. Funny thing, he always thought he was so much better than the way he played in that World Series. He said, "When I was younger, Manny, I played so much better." He was always challenging himself and his teammates.

STEVE BLASS: After the World Series [against Baltimore], we were on the team plane. [Blass pitched two complete game wins in the series. He allowed only seven hits and two runs in eighteen innings. His performance was so remarkable that he finished second in MVP voting to Clemente.] I was sitting in the window seat. Roberto came up to my aisle and gestured to me. I squeezed out of the aisle and went up to him. He said, "Let me hug you." He was so genuinely happy for me.

That's how he was. I never wanted to disappoint him.

ROBERTO CLEMENTE JR.: People saw what my dad did [Clemente hit safely in each of the seven World Series games and, in fact, hit safely in both of the World Series he played] as sort of his introduction to a large part of America. But this was a culmination of being a great player his entire life.

JUSTINO CLEMENTE WALKER: In Puerto Rico, everyone followed the three thousand hits and everyone followed the World Series. Whatever Roberto did drew the attention of all of Puerto Rico. He made everyone proud.

VERA CLEMENTE: Roberto started talking a lot about Sports City after the World Series. He wanted to use baseball to talk about the problems facing kids.

ROBERTO CLEMENTE, 1971: The World Series is the greatest thing

that ever happened to me in baseball. Mentally it has done for me
more than anything before. It
gave me a chance to talk to writers more than before. I don't
want anything for myself, but
through me I can help lots of
people. They spend millions of
dollars for dope control in Puerto
Rico. But they attack the problem after the problem is there.
Why don't they attack it before it
starts? You try to get kids so they
don't become addicts, and it
would help to get them interested in sports and give them
somewhere to learn to play them.
I want to have three baseball
fields, a swimming pool, basketball, tennis, a lake where fathers
and sons can get together . . . and
one of the biggest problems we
have today is the father doesn't
have time for the kids and they
lose control over the children.

. . . It's not enough to go to
summer camp and have one or
two instructors for a little time
and then you go home and forget

DINNER·DANCE IN HONOR OF—
ROBERTO CLEMENTE
SEPTEMBER 25, 1971
N.Y.C.

CLEMENTE

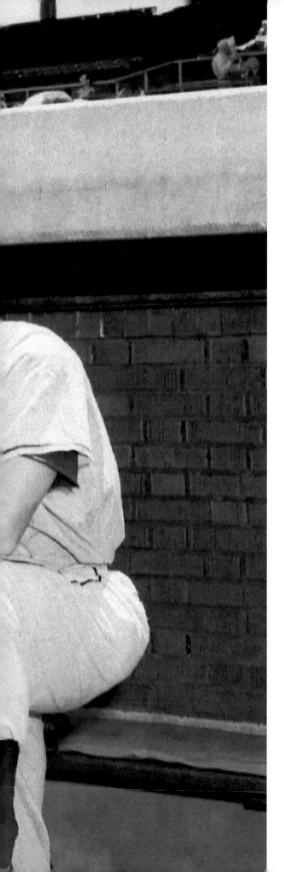

everything. You go to a Sports City and
have people like Mays and Mantle and
Williams, and kids would never forget it. I
feel the United States should have something like this all over. If I was the president of the United States I would build a
Sports City and take in kids of all ways of
life. What we want to do is exchange kids

237

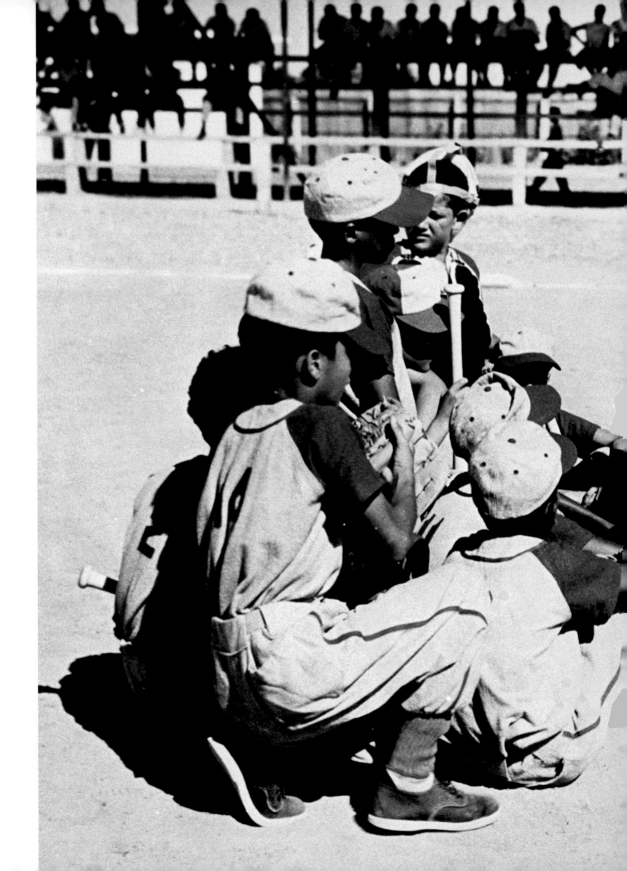

with every city in the United States and show all the kids how to live and play with other kids. [I've] been going out to different towns, different neighborhoods. I get kids together and talk about the importance of sports, the importance of being a good citizen, the importance of respecting their mother and father. I like to get together with the fathers and sons and talk to them.

Then we go to the ball field and I show them some techniques of playing baseball.

MANNY SANGUILLÉN: Puerto Rico wasn't proud of Roberto just because of what he did on the field. Puerto Ricans were proud because he always looked out for the little guy, and we were the little guy. He represented people who didn't have a voice. He used baseball to give them a voice.

CLEMENTE'S STATURE IN baseball would grow despite thorny racial politics, the occasional letter-writing psychopath, and a language barrier that hampered the early part of his career. His bat and his nobility were like antidotes. Yet as his fame grew, he never forgot three basic Clemente beliefs. These would be beliefs later embraced by his sons, with those sons teaching their children the same.

First, Clemente always paid tribute to the players who came before him. This would be the case with many other Latin and African-American players, but for Clemente it became purposeful. He'd tell his young sons, "Remember who paved the way for you." These were names like Luis Olmo or Hiram Bithorn, among a handful of others. Bithorn was the first Puerto Rican to play in the majors. A pitcher for the Chicago Cubs, he got his first victory on June 5, 1942, against the Brooklyn Dodgers. Almost a decade later, he was killed under mysterious circumstances by a Mexican policeman who stopped Bithorn and asked for his car registration while the player was traveling to see his mother for a holiday visit. In 1943, Olmo, playing for the Dodgers, became the second Puerto Rican to play professional baseball. To Clemente, these men were heroes who deserved to always be cherished, and he did exactly that. This notion has been held by many athletes of color, from Jackie Robinson to Ali to Bill Russell to Aaron to Jim Brown.

Clemente expressed two other core beliefs. He would always tell Vera, "When you are healthy and you are happy, every day of life is the same." To Clemente, every day of life was precious, and this notion would, of course, have special meaning to the family long after Clemente would say it. The second Clemente saying—that if the opportunity comes to make life better for others, and you fail to do so, then you are wasting your time in this life (what he basically told the baseball writers before the 1971 season)—would become embedded in the Clemente mitochondria. Clemente would do this with charitable acts. His widow and sons have spent their lives doing the same.

21

It was twelve-oh-five p.m. on May 14, 1973, and a remarkable man who had lived a remarkable life would affect a nation so much his legacy would be honored in one of the most prestigious places on the planet: in front of the president of the United States in the Oval Office of the White House. Actually, in what is perhaps one of the greatest validations of Roberto Clemente's charitable and baseball legacy, two U.S. presidents honored him.

It had been just five months since the plane crash. Vera was at the White House, nobly representing her husband, the beginning of a lifetime of doing so. But also in the room was President Richard Nixon, an avid sports fan, who wasn't emotionally moved by much, yet the Clemente story did move him. Nixon's place in history is well-known. What's not as well-known is how passionately he followed sports, and how he had come to adore the Clemente family following the death of Roberto.

Nixon constantly had his toe dipped in the sports world. He would write Hall of Fame coach Don Shula congratulatory letters, or call him before big games. He'd delay staff meetings if an NFL game was on, and often attended big sports events.

Though he loved football more than he did baseball, the Clemente story had caught his eye. When the idea of a Presidential Citizens Medal was forged, to Nixon and many others, Clemente was a natural choice. The medal was then, as it is now, the second-highest civilian award in the United States. The Presidential Medal of Freedom is the first.

Vera stood toward the front of the Oval Office, near Nixon, when Nixon began with some very simple words.

"Ladies and gentlemen: We are here for the presentation of the first posthumous Presidential Citizens Medal, and I am very honored and this office is honored that that first medal—which we know will be awarded in the future to distinguished Americans for their service—that first medal goes to Roberto Clemente. I would like to read the citation, because it is better than any speech I could make, I think, with regard to Roberto Clemente:

"'Citizens Medal citation, Roberto Clemente: All who saw Roberto Clemente in action, whether on the diamond or on the front lines of charitable endeavor, are richer for the experience. He stands with that handful of men whose brilliance has transformed the game of baseball into a showcase of skill and spirit, giving universal delight and inspiration. More than that, his selfless dedication to helping those with two strikes against them in life blessed thousands and set an example for millions. As long as athletes and humanitarians are honored, Roberto Clemente's memory will live; as long as Citizens Medals are presented, each will mean a little more because this first one went to him.'"

Nixon turned to a smiling Vera and presented the medal to her. Some of the Pirates players were there as well, looking on proudly. After the pause, Nixon continued.

"Let me say our only regret is that he isn't here—but he's really here—I think he is here in this room. Don't you think so? I think he would be proud to be the first American to get this medal, too, the first one."

Then began a series of speeches. Senator Hugh Scott: "Mr. President, I think the story of Roberto Clemente is too well-known for repeating, and he died, as we all

CLEMENTE

know, on a compassionate errand. In that errand, for Nicaraguan relief, he had raised, himself, a hundred and fifty thousand dollars and twenty-six tons of clothing. And it should be noted that the first contribution to that fund came from the President and Mrs. Nixon, in addition to which, very near to his heart, was the Puerto Rican sports center to which he gave much time and thought, because he believed that if kids didn't particularly like one sport while another one appealed to them, in one way or another they would get more active and learn what is to be gained from participating in that sport. So that we all are very proud of him. We all miss him, and I am glad Mrs. Clemente is here, and some of his teammates."

Then Commissioner Jaime Benítez: "I would like to say, Mr. President, on behalf of Puerto Rico, we are very honored by this occasion. We knew Clemente well and loved him as he has been loved by all of you, and we are particularly thankful to you for your great interest."

Then Nixon finished: "As you all know, ladies and gentlemen, when they do refer to the international character of this event, it should be noted that not only the Commonwealth of Puerto Rico is to benefit from it, the city of Pittsburgh, in many respects, since Roberto Clemente grew to fame in that city, but Managua in Nicaragua, one of our friends to the south. And I think that is the way Roberto Clemente would have wanted it. . . ."

In 2002, President George W. Bush would present Vera with the Presidential Medal of Freedom, the highest honor given to a civilian, in honor of Roberto. That day, this time in the East Room at the White House, Vera was joined in receiving the medal by the other recipients, who included a legendary chef, a pianist, a legendary actor, a playwright who used his talents to fight a Communist regime, a man who helped to build the first atomic bomb, a college professor, a Supreme Court justice, and a Hall of Fame basketball coach.

"Another recipient this afternoon would have been sixty-nine years old next month," Bush said at the time. "Millions of Americans remember hearing the news that Roberto Clemente had been lost on a mission to help the people of Nicaragua after an earthquake. His full name was Roberto Clemente Walker, and in an era of Mays and Mantle and Aaron, he ranked as one of the greats. He was a young man with a quick bat, a rifle arm, and a gentle heart. In the words of one baseball executive, 'I never saw any ballplayer like him. No, sir. Whenever anybody signs a big contract these days, we always wonder how many millions Clemente would be worth.' As a former team owner, it would be a lot. Yet the true worth of this man, seen in how he lived his life and how he lost his life, cannot be measured in money. And all these years later, his family can know that America cherishes the memory of Roberto Clemente."

FORMER NEW YORK CITY MAYOR RUDY GIULIANI: His deeds and actions as a humanitarian and ballplayer have inspired generations of Americans.

TONY BARTIROME: Here's what I'll mostly remember about Roberto. He was a good family man, and he really loved his three boys. He'd sometimes bring them into the clubhouse, and he always had this look in his eye when they were there. Those are the moments I'll remember most.

MANNY SANGUILLÉN: I wish he had lived longer so more people could have known him. If you got to know Roberto, you loved him.

STEVE BLASS: The things he did on the field were remarkable but it's what he did off the field that was even more impressive. I think if he were alive today, he'd be an ambassador for the sport. He'd be one of the most respected people in all of sports.

VERA CLEMENTE: One of the stories that people don't really know is something that happened when Roberto was flying once to the Dominican Republic.

There was an older woman on the flight with her daughter, and Roberto began talking to them. He liked them and said he would stay in touch with them.

A few days later on the flight back, Roberto is sitting toward the front of the plane. There's some commotion in the back and Roberto asks the [flight attendant] what's happening. There was a woman in the back of the plane who was very ill. The plane lands and he sees it was the same woman Roberto got to know on the plane ride out.

Roberto rode in the ambulance with the woman and her daughter to the hospital. She had a heart attack. While at the hospital, Roberto learned about her life and background. She had spent so much of her life helping the poor in Puerto Rico. Just as Roberto had done. Roberto told me, "She was like my mother."

The woman's last wish was to have music at her funeral. Roberto made the woman's wish come true by giving her the music.

Everything Roberto did was from the heart. Baseball . . . helping people . . . everything.

ACKNOWLEDGMENTS

The Clemente family would like to thank the fans who for decades have kept loving and admiring Roberto's memory. Fans are motivated and inspired to emulate him by becoming responsible citizens who love others. Thanks to the couples who give their newborn babies Roberto's name as a blessing, to the institutions that lend their names to various facilities and programs throughout the world, and to Major League Baseball and to Japan's Professional Baseball League for creating an award in his name to be given to the player that best exemplifies Roberto's qualities. A special mention to Liberia, Africa, for recognizing Roberto as a civil rights advocate by creating a coin in his honor. A very special thanks to Manheim, Germany, for creating the first facility to ever take his name just a few days after the accident. Thanks to our brothers from Nicaragua, for their prevailing solidarity, to the Pittsburgh fans who made it their business to spread his love and integrity to different generations, and to Roberto's former teammates for their help on this book, particularly Manny Sanguillén and Steve Blass. Thanks also to former Pirates trainer, Tony Bartirome.

A special thanks also goes to the Clemente Museum in Pittsburgh and Duane Rieder, who runs it. Also to family advisers Michael Hermann and Chuck Berry.

The writer would like to thank the Clemente family for their hospitality and graciousness during his visit to Puerto Rico, especially Luis Clemente, who patiently played tour guide.

The brain trust at Penguin Group (USA)/Celebra was diligent and thoughtful. Thank you to publisher Raymond A. Garcia and editor Brent Howard, who handled the manuscript with great skill.

Roberto Clemente often thanked and appreciated the players who came before him. If Clemente were alive, he would do the same now by thanking the Puerto Rican baseball players who helped pave the way for him to be great.

To all our family Zabala and Clemente, to our extended family—Dorsey, Garland, Coolong, Bass, Rouch, Kantrowitz, Isaac, Adrejasik, Angie Gialloretto, and Susan Wagner.

To Ramiro Martínez, Luis Rodríguez Mayoral, Benjamín Quintana, and his family.

A HUGE thank-you to Víctor "Vitín" Enríquez and Nydia Allende and her family—for always being present, from the moment of [Clemente's] disappearance to this day.

To the families of Roberto's eternal companion: Jerry Hill, Rafaél Lozano, Arthur Rivera, and Francisco Matías. We will always have you close to our hearts!

A special thanks to Puerto Rico and the people, who are proud when his name is mentioned, every time they travel, and no matter how far they go. When they say they are from Puerto Rico, they say they are from the land of Roberto Clemente. Students are inspired when they read his story; athletes feel an indescribable feeling when they represent Puerto Rico. We want to urge you to continue showcasing the values of our culture, that same culture Roberto represented and continues to represent throughout the world. May God bless you always!

NOTES

CHAPTER ONE: LOVE

18 **They became friends** Bruce Markusen, *Roberto Clemente: The Great One*, p. 10.

23 **Our conversations always** David Maraniss, *Clemente: The Passion and Grace of Baseball's Last Hero*, p. 220.

CHAPTER SIX: EMERGENCE

180 **The letter continued** Roberto Clemente FBI file number 92-6347.

CHAPTER SEVEN: PREMONITIONS

194 **"You know everything about baseball"** Bill Christine, "Remembering Roberto," *Los Angeles Times*, December 25, 1992.

EPILOGUE: 21

251 **"Ladies and gentlemen"** President Richard Nixon, transcript, the American Presidency Project.

254 **"Another recipient this afternoon"** George W. Bush, transcript, the American Presidency Project.

BIBLIOGRAPHY

Maraniss, David. *Clemente: The Passion and Grace of Baseball's Last Hero.* New York: Simon & Schuster, 2006.

Markusen, Bruce. *Roberto Clemente: The Great One.* New York: Sports Publishing LLC, 1998.

Markusen, Bruce. *The Team That Changed Baseball: Roberto Clemente and the 1971 Pittsburgh Pirates.* Yardley, PA: Westholme Publishing, 2009.

Miller, Ira. *Roberto Clemente.* New York: Tempo Books, 1973.

Musick, Phil. *Who Was Roberto?* New York: Doubleday & Company, 1974.